A Data-Driven Computer Defense

A Way to Improve Any Computer Defense

Roger A. Grimes

A Data-Driven Computer Defense: THE Computer Defense You Should Be Using

This book, like most of my others, is dedicated to my wonderful wife and best friend, Tricia. She puts up with me working way too much and understands my compulsion to help the world be a far safer place to compute. I've truly not had a bad day since I met her.

About the Author

Roger A. Grimes is a 30-year computer security consultant, instructor, holder of dozens of computer certifications, and author of 10 books and over 1,000 magazine articles on computer security. He has spoken at many of the world's biggest computer security conferences, been in *Newsweek*™ magazine, appeared on television, been interviewed for NPR's *All Things Considered*™, and been a guest on dozens of radio shows and podcasts. He has worked at some of the world's largest computer security companies, including Foundstone, McAfee, and Microsoft. He has consulted for hundreds of companies, from the largest to the smallest, around the world. He specializes in host and network security, identity management, anti-malware, hackers, honeypots, Public Key Infrastructure, cloud security, cryptography, policy, and technical writing. His certifications have included CPA, CISSP, CISA, CISM, CEH, MSCE: Security, Security+, and yada-yada others, and he has been an instructor for many of them. His writings and presentations are often known for their real-world, contrarian views. He has been the weekly security columnist for *InfoWorld* and *CSO* magazines since 2005.

Contact the Author

Email: roger@banneretcs.com

LinkedIn: https://www.linkedin.com/in/roger-grimes-b87980111/

Twitter: @rogeragrimes

CSO: https://www.csoonline.com/author/Roger-A.-Grimes/

Author's other books on Amazon:
https://www.amazon.com/Roger-A.-Grimes/e/B001IQUMT4/

Acknowledgments

Most progress is gained on the backs of previous visionaries and giants. The concepts in this book are possible only because of the prior work done by many others. I thanked many of the industry giants that I learned the most from in my previous book, *Hacking the Hacker* (Wiley).

With that said, I wish to thank the following individuals specifically for this work: Thanks to the many Chief Executive Officers (CEOs), Chief Information Security Officers (CISOs), Chief Security Officers (CSOs), military officers, and other computer security leaders who reviewed and commented on earlier versions. Thanks to Stu Sjouwerman, CEO and founder of KnowBe4, Inc., for supporting the ideas in this book early on. Thanks to former Microsoft co-workers, Joe Faulhaber and Adam Arndt, who contributed to earlier versions. Joe was living and promoting data-driven defense ideas as strongly as I was early on and shared his experiences with me during crucial stages of my development. Adam frequently gave me insight on the complex needs of risk managers. Thanks to my previous bosses, Bret Arsenault, Ahmad Mahdi, and Shahbaz Yusuf, for their encouragement and occasional course corrections when I needed them. Thanks to Shafeeq Banthanavasi, of PwC, who in a few short minutes helped me see what all security defenders ultimately wanted to get out of a data-driven report. And although not listed here individually, I sincerely appreciated my toughest critics who helped encourage me to improve my ideas and see how to put them into action. Thanks to Kelly Talbot for his professional review and editing. All of these people individually contributed into what eventually became this book. Thank you all.

A Data-Driven Computer Defense

2.0

Note: Early versions of this book were titled *A Data-Driven Computer Security Defense*. Version 2.0 incorporates new chapters, clarifications, consolidations, and more examples.

Table of Contents

Foreword

Here's a simple question. Suppose you manage the bus transit system for a large city. One of your lines, call it X, doesn't have enough buses to load all awaiting passengers, while all of your other lines are able to board those waiting. Would it be more prudent to add an additional bus or two to line X or replace all of your buses with shiny new ones?

Assuming there are no other significant issues at play, such as the need to convert to more energy-efficient buses, the answer should be a no-brainer. Yet, many companies are doing exactly the opposite when it comes to computer security. Instead of using a few resources to address the threats they actually experience, they're buying costly products that do not solve their security problems.

Things don't have to be this way, and that's why this book is so important. After explaining why security defenses are not aligned with security risks, it shows how the problem can be corrected.

Roger Grimes knows what he's talking about. He's had decades of experience helping hundreds of companies identify their security problems and determine what they need to do to fix them. He knows what works—and what doesn't.

Roger won't tell you to buy some expensive security product that won't mitigate your biggest problems. He'll show you how to spend your dollars wisely to defend against the threats you actually face.

The trick to establishing a sound security program rests on two key principles. First, base your decisions on solid data about how hackers subvert your network. Second, prioritize your threats so that you put your resources where they're most needed. The objective is to manage your risk and do so efficiently.

It won't do you any good to install the latest security gizmo if the hackers are exploiting your unpatched software. You need to know how they are getting in and align your security defenses accordingly.

This book will show you how to do that. It's also a good read.

Dorothy E. Denning

Emeritus Distinguished Professor

Naval Postgraduate School

1 Introduction

A Data-Driven Computer Defense is a common sense set of strategies to more efficiently put the right defenses in the right places in the right amounts against the right threats.

Computer War

Imagine two armies, one good, one bad, locked in a multi-decade war. The bad army is constantly winning battles on the left flank and has done so for years. In real-world battles, the good army, after noticing a weakness on the left flank, would amass more troops and resources on the left flank to counteract the enemy's continued success. In fact, in a real war, the good army would continue to amass additional resources on the left flank until it became impenetrable, or they would ultimately lose the war.

But in the virtual war that is being conducted against today's corporate computers, upon learning that the left flank is constantly being defeated, defenders inexplicably amass defending troops nearly everywhere else. They put more troops and resources on the right flank and the center. They sometimes even stack troops up vertically because they have heard of some theoretical attack from the air that they might one day have to defend against. Everyone involved can see that they are losing because of the battle occurring on the left flank, they complain about it, and then they respond by doing everything else but addressing the attacks on the left flank threat.

In a real war, if you couldn't get the generals to fight on the left flank, you would replace those generals. Unfortunately, in the computer world, those replacement generals are just as likely to concentrate on anything but the left flank, just as their predecessors did. If you think this sounds like a terrible way to conduct a war, you are right.

If you don't like the war allegory, imagine a homeowner who lives in a house that intruders constantly break into by using a window beside the door. In response, the homeowner buys more locks for his door because he's heard that most home burglaries happen because doors don't have enough locks. Or he's heard that traditional locks aren't smart enough and don't have enough technology in them. So, despite the best direct evidence that the window is the problem, the homeowner upgrades the wrong defense. Home burglars and hackers alike appreciate such a lack of appropriate focus.

Most readers will recognize parts of their companies in these allegories.

Introduction

My name is Roger A. Grimes. I've been a computer security consultant since 1987. I have dozens of computer certifications, including some of the most sought-after computer security certifications in the industry. I have been an instructor for many of them. For over 20 years, I've been a professional penetration tester, and I've broken into every company I've been hired to break into in less than three hours except for one, and that only took five hours. I've taught thousands of students around the world how to hack into computer systems and how to best defend them. I've worked for some of the world's biggest computer security companies, including Foundstone, McAfee, and Microsoft.

I've written or co-written ten books, including this one, and over 1,000 magazine articles on computer security. I have been a security columnist for *InfoWorld* or *CSO* magazine since August 2005. I am a frequently invited guest speaker at industry computer security conferences and regularly interviewed on national media shows for my sometimes contrarian and provocative views.

I've worked with hundreds of companies, large and small, and after over thirty years of experience I came to the sad conclusion that very few of them ever really did the right things at the right time with their computer security defense, even when the evidence of what they needed to do was overwhelming. In any other field, their response and approach would border on legal neglect. But this neglect wasn't on purpose and their approach doesn't need to stay this way.

This book is dedicated to explaining why most companies are inefficient defenders and how to fix the problems so that they can end up with a more efficient computer security defense that significantly lowers risk.

It is written in a friendly, first person approach, sharing examples of hard-won past experiences. A book on general computer security defense can easily be written in a staid tone. I intentionally choose a lighter, more conversational approach to give everyone a better chance of not getting bored.

Notes to Readers

There are four things to note about the writing in this book before we begin. First, I frequently use the terms *threat, risk,* and *exploit* interchangeably throughout the book, without overly focusing on their specific meaning. The context will indicate the meaning. Second, I often use the terms *corporate*, *company*, or *organization* as a stand-in for any entity that practices computer security, including a corporation, small business, organization, government agency, or military unit. Third, I often use the term *hacker* to mean malicious hacker, even though I understand that most hackers are good people who never do anything illegal or unethical. Fourth, I often use the term *computer* to mean any computer, system, or device capable of computing and being hacked, be it a computer, cell phone, laptop, Wi-Fi router, network device, etc. I use all four writing shortcuts because most readers understand what I'm trying to convey, and it just makes writing a book like this easier to write.

The Definition of Insanity

For the last 20 years, I've worked full-time reviewing companies' current security practices. I made assessments about what each was doing right and wrong, including what was badly broken. My lengthy reports have detailed the good, the bad, and the ugly. Most of the time, 80% of what the organizations were doing wrong (e.g. unpatched software, poor anti–social-engineering training, too many users in highly privileged groups, etc.) was common to almost all companies. In every case, the majority of the report came from a long boilerplate document template, with the remaining 20% being customized for each entity's peculiarities.

My reports focused on the worst negative findings and prioritized what the company could do to significantly improve their security as quickly as possible. Most of the time what I recommended as the highest criticality was low-cost and fairly easy to implement, simply an improvement or renewed focus on an already existing process. And almost every company, when I revisited later, hadn't accomplished a single critical recommendation, much less accomplished all of them.

This was true even if they had been thoroughly, publicly hacked, had lost over $100 million in damages, faced ongoing lawsuits, had CEOs and CSOs fired, and faced millions more in fines if they didn't correct the situation. Regardless of the company or direness of the situation, when I came back later, nothing that would significantly decrease their security risk had been accomplished.

It wasn't that they didn't do anything. All these companies spent a lot of money (often in the many millions of dollars) and obtained new resources (often hiring dozens of new experienced computer security employees and buying tons of new computer security services, software, and hardware), but they didn't fix the most important problems they had, even though I had spelled them out in extra-large, red, bold fonts in my reports. During report delivery, I would spend my time talking to everyone in the room and get absolute consensus on what the biggest problems were and how to fix them. Everyone would nod their heads and agree on the best solutions. And yet a year later, their biggest risks were still their biggest risks.

For example, maybe they were broken into by hackers because of unpatched Oracle Java™, and I had identified it as their biggest problem. A year later their biggest problem was still unpatched Java. They would acknowledge it, tell me all the reasons why they could not fix it, and then spend the rest of the time complaining in disbelief about why they were still being hacked so much. I would tell them it was because they didn't fix their biggest problem. They would agree. And a year would go by and still, again, nothing would be fixed. Maybe one or two companies out of hundreds over decades actually fixed their biggest problems first.

The situation I'm describing isn't unique. The problem isn't me, my findings, my reports, or my style. It happens to every computer security consultant or employee. Most long-time computer security consultants and employees go through a predictable series of shared, distinct, emotional phases in their career. They start out wanting to change the world and stop malicious hacking. They are euphoric, eager, and ready to put in the long hours that it takes to make the world a better place. I liken their optimistic attitudes to new teachers or nurses.

Unfortunately, they end up being disappointed by the realization that the hackers will very likely always win. They are quickly frustrated by being forced to work on projects that will not do much to significantly reduce hacking trouble. They might even know what they need to do to really significantly reduce risk, but they aren't allowed to do it. They are responsible for everything and given none of the authority to fix it. It's torturous. It depresses them and breaks down their enthusiasm.

After a few years, nearly every computer security employee ends up feeling that they can't really stop attackers and the best they can do is to keep their head down and focus on doing what they are told to do, even if what they are doing won't really help that much.

I have counseled dozens of computer security professionals who are frustrated with their careers. Some accept their occupation for what it is. Others simply give up and switch careers into something else entirely because they cannot live with how soul-crushing and unfulfilling it can be.

The front-line computer security defenders blame management for not listening to them, and senior management keeps wondering why their millions of dollars are not making their entities more resistant to attack. Senior management is often resigned to feeling like they are trying to survive until the likely day when hackers penetrate their defenses and even higher senior management asks them to fall on their own sword. Everyone on the team is demoralized to a certain extent.

The end result of most corporate computer defense strategies is that hackers can easily penetrate enterprise defenses at will, negating all those millions of spent dollars and "brilliant" strategies. Most of today's defenses work so poorly that the entire industry of corporate defenders is being told that the only way to even minimize the problem ("because you can't stop it!") is to adopt an "Assume Breach" style of defense.

Assume Breach believes the hacker is already inside your porous defenses or easily could be. This isn't hyperbole. It's the reality for most organizations. And so, you need to beef up early detection alerts and implement defenses to isolate and slow down hackers and malware once they are on the inside.

The sad reality is that most of these organizations aren't doing the simple, usually less expensive, things that would make their environments significantly more secure and more difficult to successfully attack.

An outside observer watching this misaligned chaos might mistakenly conclude that all these complaining, attacked companies aren't doing anything to defend themselves from the initial attacks. They might even come to believe that these companies must want to be successfully attacked. Such an observer could be forgiven for coming to such conclusions because that's what it looks like when you see how most companies are not correctly responding to their biggest threats.

With a different approach that clearly defines the biggest threats and focuses on the right things, the companies would be better secured and IT security employees would be happier. This book is about finding that better place.

The Problem and the Solution

Many companies do not appropriately align computer security defenses with the threats that pose the greatest risk (i.e. damage) to their environment. After I recognized the central problem, I spent nearly a decade trying to figure out why this was true. After all, no one wants to waste time and money on strategies that are doomed to fail. No one wants to resign their career to the fact that they will never win or be successful. No one wants to make poor choices. But nearly everyone is doing so. How did things get this way?

After reevaluating hundreds of security reviews that I had performed over decades and speaking with over a hundred CSOs and hundreds of front-line computer security employees, I was able to recognize common patterns and problems. I address them in Chapter 3, "Broken Defenses". They all share one outcome—they lead corporations to focus on the wrong things.

The best computer security consultants recognize that there is a world-sized gap between the myriad of critical threats you are told to fear and the biggest successful threats you ACTUALLY currently have and will most likely need to deal with in the near future. If you truly understand that distinction and all of its ramifications, you can probably skip a third of this book, even though I think you'll enjoy reading more of the context. Either way, I'll revisit this concept in a variety of ways throughout this book.

The growing number of ever-evolving threats has made it more difficult for organizations to identify and appropriately rank the risk of their most critical threats, especially against each other. This leads to an inefficient and often ineffective application of security controls—at least in the right places in the right amounts.

The implementation weaknesses described in this book are common to most organizations and point to limitations in traditional modeling of computer security threats. Most of the inefficiency occurs due to inaccurate risk ranking and poor communications and leads to uncoordinated, slow, ineffectual responses.

Chapter 4, "Fixing Broken Defenses", proposes a solution framework that can help organizations more efficiently allocate defensive resources against the most likely threats in the right places in the right amounts to better reduce risk. As discussed in Chapter 10, "Selling DDD", this new data-driven approach to a computer security defense plan results in many benefits, including:

- Increased focus on the right things

- Improved data collection and analysis

- More efficient, lower cost, computer security defense

- Better threat intelligence

- Improved threat detection

- Quicker responses to growing threats

- Reduced damage

- More accountability

- Measurably lower computer security risk

- Increased trust in computer security defenses

- Improved morale for all stakeholders

The key goal of an implemented Data-Driven Computer Defense is to more accurately align and funnel mitigations against the root causes of the most successful, damaging threats. The outcome is a more efficient appropriation of defensive resources with measurably lower risk. The measure of success of a data- and relevancy-driven computer defense is fewer high-risk compromises and faster responses to successful exploits.

If such a defense is implemented correctly, defenders will focus on the most critical initial-compromise exploits that are most likely to harm their organization. It will efficiently reduce risk more quickly than other defense strategies and appropriately align resources. And when the next new threat vector lifecycle begins, the organization can recognize it earlier and respond and reduce damage more quickly.

Reprogramming Your Brain and Culture

Following a Data-Driven Computer Defense involves impacting every part of the organization, not just the computer security or IT departments. That alone is difficult enough, but it becomes even more so because many of the things I'm going to tell you to do will seem like the antithesis of what you've been taught your entire professional life. You, your co-workers, and your bosses will likely be skeptical at first. That is normal and to be expected until you and they see the results.

Whenever you have a huge, long-term structural problem that isn't being solved by traditional means, it requires a paradigm shift in thinking, often across an entire industry or the larger culture. It wouldn't be a big, long-standing, problem in the first place if it didn't require a big shift that can sometimes feel wrong at first. What years later is eventually recognized as common sense can initially feel counterintuitive.

For example, in the nutrition industry, it's taken decades of empirical studies to demonstrate that sugar and carbs may be causing more problems than fat and that eating whole eggs doesn't cause cholesterol problems. Yet, most of the diet advice still is based on the notion that eating fat makes you fat and eating eggs gives you cholesterol, even though nearly every study coming out today does not show that to be true.

The New Password Paradigm

Many paradigm shifts are occurring in the computer security industry right now. For example, we all know that one of the best things you can do for a good computer security defense is to enforce that all users use strong passwords. Strong passwords must be long (at least 12 characters), be complex (incorporating multiple types of character sets: uppercase, lowercase, numbers, and symbols), and be frequently changed with a maximum life of 90 days. That is a well-known fact supported by every computer security leader. There isn't a computer security regulation or best practice that doesn't say this. A strong password policy is often required by regulatory law (e.g. PCI-DSS, SOX, HIPAA, NERC, etc.).

However, decades of experience and data shows this approach is wrong and likely contributes to an increase in successful malicious attacks. Yep. Everything you've ever heard about password policy in the past is wrong. Today's most knowledgeable password experts now recommend non-complex passwords that rarely change. Anything else probably increases your risk. Frustratingly, it will probably take another half decade or longer for the existing computer security guidelines and laws to be updated to reflect the better methods. So, you'll probably be forced to implement the old requirements for many years to come even though it actually increases your security risk.

A former co-worker of mine at Microsoft Corporation, Dr. Cormac Herley, is on the forefront of the new recommended password policies. When he and others looked at the data, they found out that the data on password hacks did not support the old best practice recommendations. Updated research and a renewed look at the data turned the computer security world upside down regarding password policy.

It's not as if the new password policies are a secret. They can be found in the world's most trustworthy sites for computer security policy, including https://pages.nist.gov/800-63-3/sp800-63b.html and https://www.microsoft.com/en-us/research/wp-content/uploads/2016/06/Microsoft_Password_Guidance-1.pdf. When these policies came out, their contrarian ideas made headlines for weeks around the world. It was the opposite of being a secret. Still, most people, including most of the readers of this book, haven't heard of them. Ideas that run contrary to long-held beliefs take a long time to become generally accepted, even if the data is better and many people broadcast it to the world.

As Cormac said in my book, *Hacking the Hacker* (https://www.amazon.com/Hacking-Hacker-Learn-Experts-Hackers/dp/1119396212/), "I didn't come into the computer security world to intentionally and deliberately antagonize anyone. But because I've only recently come into the security world, I didn't have the long-standing culture biases that many others get. I had a different background, driven by data and the need to see supporting data. When I didn't see good data, it allowed me to ask fundamental questions, which the culture had already long accepted. I wanted to get the data, test, and do the empirical analysis—do things with math. It's not only a desirable way of doing things, but necessary. You might have a model of how you think 2 billion users will behave but 2 billion users will respond the way they are going to respond regardless of your model. You can hope that it happens, but you have to measure what happens to see if there is any resemblance to what happened [to compare] to your model. And if your model is wrong, change it."

Security by Obscurity Is Good

Here's another example: Most computer security practitioners are taught early on that "security by obscurity is no security." The idea is that attackers might be able to discover any fact surrounding your system, so assume they have all the necessary facts and design your security system to be secure even if they have perfect knowledge of it (for everything but the ultimate authentication secrets). The "security by obscurity is no security" dogma is believed and repeated so much that it borders on religion. However, it isn't any truer than the old password policy beliefs.

The truth is that obscurity is a great defense and often one of the best ways to get the biggest bang for your security dollar. It just shouldn't be the only or primary way your system is secured. You should still design a system as if the axiom is true. It can only help you. But there is a fundamental difference between not relying solely on security by obscurity and refusing to benefit from it at all.

If you look at the data, you should absolutely include some obscurity as part of your overall security defense. Any variable that a hacker has to guess or look for slows them down and makes their job harder. If obscurity is no security, then why don't the world's armies tell each other where their nuclear subs are traveling and where all the nuclear missile silos are located? I can tell you why. Obscurity has good security value.

Throughout this book I'm going to ask you to question some of your existing beliefs. I'm going to offer you new ways to look at things that have always been right before your very eyes. But instead of just asking you to blindly accept what I say or even giving you someone else's data, I'm going to ask you to use your own data and experiences. In fact, this whole book is about gathering your own data to build your best possible computer security defense. No one else's data means as much as the data from your own, localized experience. When you get through with this book, you should always be skeptical of other people's data, especially the further it gets away from your own organization's current experiences.

Some of this book will seem overly defensive at times, especially when discussing how to "sell" these ideas to others in Chapter 10, "Selling DDD". That's because I know what a "hard sell" it can be to others who are not ready to accept the basic facts. It is my greatest hope that one day everything said in this book is accepted as common sense, because it is common sense. But in the end, the only proof that matters is your organization experiencing less damage from current and future attacks. Everything else is opinion.

> "If I were to try to read, much less answer, all the attacks made on me, this shop might as well be closed for any other business. I do the very best I know how—the very best I can; and I mean to keep doing so until the end. If the end brings me out all right, what is said against me won't amount to anything. If the end brings me out wrong, ten thousand angels swearing I was right would make no difference."—Abraham Lincoln

This Book's Chapters

This book is broken down into ten chapters that are spread across three main parts.

Part I, "Bad Defenses"

This part of the book talks about Data-Driven Computer Defense, the methods hackers use to compromise systems, and how most of today's corporations are doing computer security defense wrong and why.

Chapter 1, "Introduction"

This chapter introduces the data-driven computer defense concept and why it is needed.

Chapter 2, "How and Why Hackers Hack"

Most hackers follow a general series of common, sequential steps to compromise a system, even if they don't always use all of the steps or use them in the same order. Understanding how hackers and their malware break into systems is essential to stopping them.

Chapter 3, "Broken Defenses"
Companies don't want to defend poorly, so why do they do so? This chapter explains what they are doing wrong and how security got to be this way. The first step in fixing a problem is admitting you have a problem.

Part II, "A Better Data-Driven Defense"
This part of the book explains the theory behind a data-driven defense and gives all the details for why it is the right way for any organization to improve their computer defense efficiency.

Chapter 4, "Fixing Broken Defenses"
This chapter discusses the key elements for creating a better defense that more efficiently aligns mitigations against the right threats.

Chapter 5, "A DDD Example"
This chapter uses data-driven computer defense strategies to reinvent and improve a very common computer defense, patch management, as an example to help you to start thinking in a data-driven way.

Chapter 6, "Asking the Right Questions"
This chapter discusses how defenders need to ask better questions to get to the crux of their computer security problems.

Chapter 7, "Getting Better Data"
This chapter tells you how to obtain better data to more accurately drive your new computer security defense.

Part III, "Implementing a Data-Driven Defense"
In most cases, changing to a Data-Driven Computer Defense means impacting the whole corporate culture, changing focus, and affecting every part of the organization. It's not easy. This part of the book tells you how to do it, especially because every organization is unique and requires a custom solution.

Chapter 8, "The Data-Driven Computer Defense Lifecycle"
This chapter helps you drive all the new lifecycle components of a data-driven defense within your own corporate culture.

Chapter 9, "More Implementation Examples"
This chapter gives example after example of the ways different companies implemented a better data-driven defense. Most of the examples cited here can be implemented within your own organization.

Chapter 10, "Selling DDD"
This chapter tells how to get your company to accept a data-driven computer defense across the entire organization. It summarizes the benefits and arguments any DDD proponent can use to sell this new data-driven methodology and provides step-by-step recommendations any company can use to implement a DDD mindset and plan across their entire organization.

The theories and approaches described in this book have now been put into practice across dozens of companies with great success. Since version 1.0 of this book was released, it has sold more than 30,000 copies, and dozens of companies have thanked me for the positive impact on their organization's computer defense plans. They are all proof-positive examples of the practical risk reduction strategies shared in this book.

The best part of this success is that these new corporate cultures now think of data-driven defense as common sense. It is a part of their ethos. The old way seems non-sensical. It just took some data, a few examples, and a little prodding to see what was working and why in order to get to the new understanding.

This Book Is a Red Pill

In the popular 1999 movie, *The Matrix*, the protagonist, Neo, is shown the terrible reality that exists under the false surface that he perceives. At a pivotal point in the movie, he is offered a red pill and a blue pill. The red pill will keep him forever awakened to reality, no matter how painful and challenging that new reality will be. But he can instead choose to take the blue pill, which will render him back into his original, more tranquil ignorance. Neo takes the red pill and reclaims his world from its robot overlords.

This book is your red pill. If I'm successful, from this moment forward you will forever think differently about computer security. You will see most computer defenses for what they are: inefficient, incorrectly ranked, and wastes of money and resources. You will no longer accept unranked items of things to do. Instead of blindly accepting dogma, you will require data to back it up. You will only value other people's data after you measure and weigh it against your own data and experiences. Gut feelings are great. Data-driven defenses are divine. Have no doubt about it: My goal is to change the way you see and think about computer security for the rest of your life.

If you have any questions or comments, please don't hesitate to email me at roger@banneretcs.com. Keep up the good fight!

2 How and Why Hackers Hack

In order to protect against malicious hackers, defenders need to understand their methods. Chapter 2 discusses the general techniques and methodology that hackers use to compromise computer systems and networks.

> *"The 'many eyes' theory of efficiently finding software bugs doesn't work for the same reason asking a bunch of airline passengers to inspect a plane for all known defects doesn't."*—Unknown

Hackers and their motivations may widely vary, but hacking techniques don't substantially differ, regardless of whether they're being implemented by some lazy slob sipping on an energy drink in their bedroom at night or a state-sponsored professional.

Hackers vs. Hollywood

Hollywood has made the world think that computer hackers are these god-like, uber-geniuses who can break into any computer they feel like in under a minute. They can guess any password in a few seconds, especially if their boss is yelling at them or puts a gun to their head.

The reality is that most hackers are very normal people with normal intelligence. What most hackers have in above-average quantities are the curiosity to see how things work beyond the normally presented interface and the persistence to try nearly the same thing over and over, sometimes for weeks, to reach their goal. Hackers handle immediate frustration better than most people.

A hacker is similar to a tradesperson, like a plumber or electrician. They understand and use the right tools and methodologies in the right places. But instead of using the right screwdriver or wrench, they use the appropriate hacking tool for the job.

Most hackers follow a common methodology of standard steps, whether they realize it or not. Not all hackers use all the steps. Some hackers only use one step. But in general, if someone follows all the steps, they are more likely to be successful at hacking. I've taught thousands of students around the world how to hack into anything they want by following the hacker methodology.

A hacker can skip one or more of the steps and still be a successful hacker. Malware and other hacking tools often allow hackers to skip steps, but at least one of the steps, the initial penetration foothold, is always required. It is what makes a hacker a hacker. And defeating that step is crucial to a data-driven defense.

The Hacking Methodology

If you're going to fight malicious hackers or their malware creations, you have to understand the "hacking methodology" or whatever it is being called by the person or document describing it. The model can vary depending on who is describing it, including the number of steps, what is involved in each step, and the names of each of the steps, but all the models contain the same basic components.

The hacking methodology contains the following generally progressive steps:

1. Information Gathering
2. Initial Foothold Penetration
3. Optional: Guaranteeing Easier Future Access
4. Optional: Internal Reconnaissance
5. Optional: Movement
6. Intended Action Execution
7. Optional: Covering Tracks

Let's examine each hacker methodology in more detail.

Information Gathering

Unless a hacker tool is helping the hacker to randomly access any possible vulnerable site, the hacker usually has a destination target, or set of targets, in mind. If a hacker wants to penetrate a specific system, the first thing the hacker does is start researching everything they can about the systems and networks that might possibly help them break in.

At the very least, this means domain names, IP addresses, email addresses, naming conventions, and user names. The hacker finds out how many potential sites and services they can access that are connected to the target. They can use the Internet or other public information to find out employee names for social engineering. The hacker might look up news stories to see what big software program or cloud service the target has bought recently, what mergers or divestures are happening (these are always messy affairs often accompanied by relaxed or missed security), and even what partners and relying parties the company interacts with. Many companies have been compromised through a much weaker partner or subcontractor.

Finding out what digital assets a company is connected to is the most important part of information gathering in most hacker attacks. Not only are the main (public) sites and services usually identified, but it's usually more helpful to the attacker to find the less popular connected sites and services, like employee and partner portals. The less popular sites and servers are more likely to have a weakness compared to the main sites that other hackers have already been beating on for years.

Then any good hacker starts to gather all the software and services hosted on each of those sites, a process generally known as *fingerprinting*. It's very important to learn what operating systems (OSs) are used and what versions. OS versions can tell a hacker what patch levels and bugs may or may not be present. For example, they might find Microsoft Windows Server 2016™ and Linux Red Hat CentOS™ 7.2-1613. Then they look for software programs and their versions (for the same reason) running on each OS. If it's a web server, they might find Internet Information Server™ 7 on the Microsoft Windows 2013 R2 Server™ and Apache 2.6.2 on the Red Hat Enterprise Linux™ server.

They create an inventory of each device, OS, application, and version running on each of their intended targets. It's always best to make a complete inventory to get an inclusive picture of the target's landscape, but other times a hacker may find a big vulnerability early on and just jump into the next step. Outside of such a quick exploit, usually the more information the hacker has about what is running, the better. Each additional software and version provides further possible attack vectors.

Sometimes when a hacker connects to the service or site, it helpfully responds with very detailed version information so they don't need any tools. When that isn't the case, there are plenty of tools, like Nmap (https://nmap.org/) to help with the OS fingerprinting and Nikto2 (https://cirt.net/Nikto2) to assist with web server application fingerprinting. Either way, a successful hacker usually has to have basic information about the system they are trying to break into, and the more information, the better, before beginning the next, most important step.

Initial Foothold Penetration

This is the step that puts the "hack" in "hacker"—gaining initial foothold access (aka *initial exploit*). The success of this step makes or breaks the entire cycle. If the hacker has done their homework in the previous fingerprinting stage, then this stage really isn't all that hard. There is always old software being used, always something left unpatched, and almost always something misconfigured in the collection of identified software.

If, by chance, all the software and devices are perfectly secured (and they rarely are), a hacker can wait for a new related exploit to be announced, discover a new one themselves, or attack the human element, which is often the weakest part of the equation. But without the initial penetrating foothold, all is lost for the hacker.

Fortunately for the hacker, there are lots of ways to penetrate a target, including:

- Programming Bug
- Social Engineering
- Authentication Attack
- Human Error
- Misconfiguration
- Eavesdropping/MitM
- Data/Network Traffic Malformation
- Insider Attack
- Reliance Issues
- Physical Attack

Note: It is my intention for this list to be an inclusive list of possible, distinct, hacking methods. However, I recognize that this list of hacking methods could be incomplete or better described by different classifications. This list is intended to be my best summary at the time of this writing. It has changed since the first edition of this book and will likely continue to evolve in the future.

Programming Bug

A programming bug is an error or mistake introduced in the coding process while creating a software, firmware, or hardware program or set of instructions which can result in unintended malicious actions or access. The error can be introduced by the developer, the development process, or the tools involved. The programming bug may be unknown to anyone, known by one or a few people, or publicly released and made known to everyone in the communications channel.

If the programing bug is known, an update (e.g. patch, software update, etc.) may be available to fix the vulnerability. Since the beginning of computers, one of the most common hacker compromise methods is accessing a system using a known vulnerability that the user or administrator has yet to patch.

Vendors have generally gotten better at writing more secure code and finding their own bugs before external hackers do, but there are an ever-increasing number of programs and billions of lines of code, so the overall number of publicly known bugs has risen over time.

Most vendors do a fairly good job of patching their software in a timely manner, especially after a vulnerability becomes publicly known. Unfortunately, customers are notoriously slow in applying those patches, even often going so far as disabling the vendor's own auto-patching routines. Some surprising percentage of users never patch their system. The user either ignores the multiple patch warnings and sees them as purely annoying or is completely unaware that a patch needs to be applied. (For example, many point-of-sale systems don't notify cashiers that a patch needs to be applied.) Most software exploits happen to software that has not been patched in many, many years.

Even if a particular company or user patches critical vulnerabilities as quickly as possible after they are announced, a persistent, patient hacker can just wait for a patch to be announced that is on their target's fingerprint inventory list and launch the related attack before the defender has time to apply the patch. (It's relatively easy for a hacker to reverse engineer patches and find out how to exploit a particular vulnerability.)

A special subset of programming bugs is known as *zero-days*. Zero-days (or *0-days*) are exploits accomplished by an attacker for which no public knowledge or patch is available. Zero-days are less common than everyday vulnerabilities that have been publicly revealed and vendors have usually patched, although this has changed regarding the Microsoft Windows platform starting in 2017. Any computer system using software with a zero-day bug is essentially exploitable at-will, unless the potential victim uninstalls the software or has put in place some sort of other defensive mitigation (for example a firewall, ACL list, VLAN segmentation, virtual patch filter, anti-buffer overflow software, and so on).

Zero-days are not as common as known exploits because they can't be widely used by an attacker. If an attacker overused a zero-day, the coveted exploit hole would be discovered, publicly revealed, and patched by vendors. These days most vendors can patch new exploits within a few hours to a few days after discovery.

When zero-days are used, either they are used very broadly against many targets all at once for maximum exploitation potential or they are used "low and slow" in targeted attacks, which means sparingly and only when absolutely needed. The world's best professional hackers usually have collections of zero-days that they use only when all else has failed and even then in such a way that they won't likely be noticed. A zero-day might be used to gain an initial foothold in an especially resistant target, and then all traces of its use will be removed and more traditional methods will be used from that point onward.

Social Engineering

One of the most successful hacking strategies is social engineering. Social engineering, whether accomplished manually by a human adversary or done using automation, is any hacker or malware ruse that relies upon tricking an end-user into doing something detrimental to their own computer or security. It can be an email that tricks an end-user into clicking on a malicious web link or running a rogue file attachment. It can be something or someone deceiving a user into revealing their private logon information (called phishing).

Social engineering is so easy and has such a high chance of success that when I was a penetration tester, I used to get disappointed if a client wanted us to use it during a test. Social engineering provided such quick and sure results that it took all the challenge out of penetration testing. It was just too easy.

Authentication Attack

Authentication is the process of a subject (e.g. user, device, group, service, daemon, etc.) providing proof of ownership of an identity to an underlying security access control system. If the proof is sufficient, the system trusts that the subject is who they say they are, and the subject can then be assigned the associated predefined permissions and privileges to the system or software.

Authentication attacks take advantage of weaknesses or vulnerabilities in the underlying authentication system or process to gain unauthorized access. Authentication system attacks can involve the unauthorized access to passwords (and their derivatives), access control systems and tokens, and multi-factor authentication devices and software.

Password guessing and cracking used to comprise the majority these attacks, but password hash, credential theft, and reuse attacks (such as *pass-the-hash* attacks) have become the biggest portion of this attack type over the last decade. With credential theft attacks, an attacker usually gains administrative access to a computer and retrieves one or more logon credentials stored on the system (either in memory or on the longer-term storage media). The stolen credentials are then used to access other systems that accept the same logon credentials.

Almost every major corporate attack in the last decade has involved credential theft attacks as a common exploit component, so much so that traditional password guessing isn't as popular anymore. This change in password hacking is one of the primary reasons that password policy recommendations have recently changed, as discussed in the previous chapter.

Human Error

When it comes to initial foothold penetration, human error is any unintended action that results in unauthorized access to software, systems, networks, or data. According to the Privacy Rights Clearinghouse Data Breaches repository (https://www.privacyrights.org/data-breaches), the largest and longest-public service dedicated to tracking data breaches, human error is one of the most common reasons for malicious compromise. Examples include the following:

- Unauthorized persons are unintentionally sent the wrong information.

- Private records are left behind after a move to a new location.
- Private records are thrown away and discovered by "dumpster divers".
- Unencrypted USB keys containing private data are lost or stolen.

Misconfiguration

Misconfiguration is a special class of human error. It is fairly common for computer users and administrators to (sometimes inadvertently) implement very weak security choices. Many compromises are due to a software or operating system security choice that has weakened security below more secure settings. These weaker settings often go against the vendor's defaults and best practice recommendations of computer security organizations.

I can't tell you how many times I've gone to a company-wide file repository or even public web site to find that its most critical files are somehow marked with Everyone or World Full Control permissions—and those permissions are exactly what they look like. Some misconfigurations are done unintentionally. Other misconfigurations are done intentionally but without the responsible party being fully aware of the unwanted future consequences. Sometimes it is simply due to mistakes, such as an administrator intending to temporarily disable a firewall or assign broad admin permissions during a troubleshooting event and then later forgetting to undo the change.

Eavesdropping/MitM

Eavesdropping and *"man-in-the-middle"* (*MitM*) attacks compromise a network connection to gain access to or maliciously participate in the communications between two or more authorized parties. Most eavesdropping occurs due to flaws in network or application protocols, but it can also be accomplished due to human error. These days, the biggest eavesdropping attacks occur on wireless networks or on web site connections, especially when social engineering is involved.

Data/Network Traffic Malformation

Data and network traffic malformation attacks are when an attacker intentionally malforms data or traffic in such a way as to cause an otherwise unintended action or access. Common examples of malforming data are buffer overflow and SQL injection attacks.

Malformation of network traffic is often used to cause service and availability disruptions to legitimate users. Denial of service (DoS) attacks work by overwhelming one or more computing processes with large amounts of forged information. DoS attacks are notoriously difficult to defend against. Today, even if every computing asset in a system is hardened against DOS attacks, enormous distributed denial of service (DDoS) attacks, sending hundreds of billions of forged network packets per second, can still take networks and computers down.

Even if your computers are perfectly secured against mass DDoS attacks, they probably rely on one or more external services that are not under your control and are not perfectly secure. For example, DDoS attacks can take down the DNS services your site depends on. Or your ISP. Huge networks have had to drop targeted customers simply because they could not sustain a huge DDoS attack directed against a single web site on their network to the detriment of all the other co-located customers.

There are dozens of commercial (sometimes illegal) services that anyone can use to both cause and defend against huge DDoS attacks. Each year, many vendors under DDoS attack pay the attacker a ransom to avoid or stop the attack. For them, it's worth paying the ransom versus the monetary damage the DDoS attack would otherwise cause. Some very unscrupulous anti-DDoS vendors have been found to actually instigate DDoS attacks to gain customers, which is like paying the mob to stay in business.

Insider Attack

Insider attacks are instances of unauthorized actions or access by trusted employees, consultants, and other known and trusted third parties. The insiders can have all the necessary permissions and privileges to carry out their unauthorized actions or use social engineering methods to gain the credentials or access capabilities of others. Insider attacks have always been a significant concern for organizations.

Reliance Issues

Most organizations rely on access, data, and interfaces under the control of or used by other organizations. If the trusted organization, process, data, or tool being relied upon is compromised, it can often be used to compromise the original, trusting, organization.

For example, one large organization had its global operations compromised and damage in the tens of millions of dollars resulted because its refrigeration maintenance vendor used weak passwords on remote access control units that were meant to manage the refrigeration systems. Another organization was compromised because its security web cameras were exploited and then used to capture typed-in passwords to other critical control systems.

Perhaps the best example of a reliance attack was the Stuxnet worm in 2010 (https://en.wikipedia.org/wiki/Stuxnet). In the original Stuxnet attack, Russian engineers' USB keys were (unknowingly) compromised in order to infect and destroy Iranian nuclear fuel centrifuges. The rise of Internet of Things (IoT) devices will only increase reliance issues and their unintended consequences.

The difference between an insider attack and a reliance issue is intent. An insider intends to do something unauthorized, whereas reliance risk is due to unintended consequences.

Physical Attack

A physical attack is any cyberattack requiring physical access to the system, device, or software being exploited. Conventional wisdom says that if an attacker has physical access to a computer, they can just steal the whole thing (poof, your cell phone is gone), destroy it, or bypass all protections to access private data. And this perception has proven pretty accurate so far, even against defenses that are explicitly meant to protect against physical attacks.

For example, many disk encryption programs can be defeated by the attacker using an electron microscope to identify the protected secret key by distinguishing the individual electrons that compose the key. Or RAM chips can be frozen by canned air and examined to reveal the secret encryption key stored on them in plaintext because of the way common computer memory physically stores data. Physical attacks are very difficult to prevent.

Privilege Escalation

Each hacker uses one of the various penetration methods described in the previous sections to initially exploit a target system. The only question after gaining initial access is what type of security access they get. If they exploit a software program or service running in the exploited user's own security context, they initially only have the same access privileges and permissions as the user. Or they may get the holy grail on that system and get complete administrative system access.

If the attacker only gets regular, non-privileged user access permissions, then they generally execute a second, "privilege escalation" attack to try to obtain higher privileged access. Privilege escalation attacks run the gamut, essentially duplicating the same approaches as for initial penetration, but they begin with the higher base starting point of already having at least some system access. Privilege escalation attacks are generally easier to perform than the initial exploits. And since the initial exploits are almost always guaranteed to succeed, the privilege escalation is just that much easier.

Guaranteeing Easier Future Access

Although it's optional, once an attacker has obtained the initial foothold access, most hackers then work on implementing an additional method to ensure that they can more easily access the same asset or software faster the next time around. For many hackers, this means placing a "listening" backdoor program that they can directly connect to next time. Other times it means cracking passwords or creating new accounts. The attacker can always use the same exploits that worked successfully last time to gain the initial foothold, but they usually they want some other method that will work even if the victim fixes the issue that worked previously.

Internal Reconnaissance

Once hackers have penetrated the system, they can start executing multiple commands or programs to learn more about the target they have gained access to and what things are connected to it. Usually that means looking in memory, on the hard drive, for network connectivity, and enumerating users, shares, services, and programs. All this information is used to better understand the target and also as a launching point for the next phase of attacks.

Movement

It is the rare attacker or malware program that is content to break into one target. Nearly all hackers and malware programs want to spread their range of influence over more and more targets. Once they gain access to the initial target, spreading that influence within the same network or entity is pretty easy. The hacker penetration methods listed in this chapter summarize the various ways they can do it, but comparing it to the initial foothold efforts, the subsequent movement is easier.

If the attacker moves to other similar targets with similar uses, it is called lateral movement. If the attacker moves from devices of one privilege level to a higher or lower privilege or to different uses, it's called vertical movement. Most attackers move from lower to high levels of privilege using vertical movement techniques (again, using the hacker penetration methods described in this chapter). Some organizations call the series of sequential steps a hacker or malware program implements the "exploit chain" or "kill chain".

For example, a very common hacker exploit chain is for the attacker to first compromise a single, regular end-user workstation. They use that initial foothold to search for and download local administrative account passwords. Then, if those local administrative credentials are shared among more machines (which they often are), they then move across the network to other hosts, repeating the process until they can capture privileged account access. Sometimes this is done immediately during the first break-in because the logged-on user or system already has very high privileges. They then move to the authentication server and capture every user's logon credentials. This is the standard modus operandi for most hacker groups these days, and moving from the initial compromise to complete network ownership (or "pwning" in hacker terminology) can be accomplished in less than an hour.

Intended Action Execution

After access is gained, hackers (or malware) then pull off whatever they intend to do. Every hacker has intent. A legitimate penetration tester has a contractual obligation to do one or more things. A malicious hacker might spread malware, read or steal confidential information, make a malicious modification, eavesdrop, or cause some sort of damage.

In the old days (two or three decades ago), simply showing off that they had hacked a system would have been enough for most hackers. Today, most hacking is 99% criminally motivated, and the hacker is going to do something malicious to the target (even if the only damage they do is to remain silently infiltrated for some potential future action). Unauthorized access without any direct damage is still damage.

Some malware is originally programmed to accomplish some specific intention. Other malware programs exist only to get an initial foothold in a system and then "dial home" to receive any of a variety of further instructions or to download a longer persisting malware program. These programs are known by many names, including *downloaders*. The controlling systems they connect back to are known as *command and control C&C)*. The process of connecting to a C&C infrastructure is often done dozens of times before the final intended malware program and/or instructions of intent are received. Regardless of whether the attacker is an auto-updating program or a hacker, it is the rare that they don't anything other than break in.

Covering Tracks

Some hackers and malware programs will try to hide or delete evidence of their existence or actions. This used to be what almost all hackers did years ago, but these days computer systems are so complex and in such great numbers that most computer owners don't check for hacker tracks. They don't check the logs, they don't check the firewall, and they don't look for any sign of illegal hacking unless it hits them in the face.

Each year, the *Verizon Data Breach Investigations Report* (http://www.verizonenterprise.com/verizon-insights-lab/dbir/) reports that most attackers go unnoticed for months to years, even though over 80% of the attacks would have been noticed had the defenders bothered to look. Because of this reality, most hackers and malware programs don't bother to cover their tracks anymore.

Hackers need to cover their tracks even less these days because they are using methods such as traditional legitimate admin tools and script languages, which will never be detected with traditional hacker-event detection. Hackers often use things that are so common in the victim's environment that it becomes nearly impossible to distinguish between legitimate and illegitimate activity.

For example, after breaking in, a hacker usually performs actions in the security context of a legitimate user, often accessing the same servers and services as the legitimate user does. And they use the same tools (such as remote access software and scripting languages) that the admins do. Who can easily tell what is and isn't malicious?

Hacking Is a Repeatable Process

If you wanted to know how hackers hack, there you go. It's all summarized in the preceding sections. The only thing left to do is add tools, curiosity, and persistence. The hacking cycle works so well that many penetration testers, after getting over their initial excitement at being paid to be a professional hacker, get bored and move on to something else after a few years. Could there be a bigger testament to how well the cycle works than that it becomes boring? And it is within this framework and understanding that defenders need to fight against attackers.

Automated Malware as a Hacking Tool

When malware is involved, it can accomplish one or more of the hacking steps, automate everything, or hand over manual control to a hacker once the target is acquired and pwned. Most hacking groups use a combination of social engineering, automated malware, and human attackers to accomplish their objectives. In larger groups, the individual hackers may have assigned roles and specialties. Malware is often similar to hacker groups, with different programs performing different roles in different points of the exploitation chain.

Or malware may execute a single penetration step and be successful without ever trying any of the other steps. For example, the fastest malware program in history, SQL Slammer, was just 376 bytes. That's miniscule compared to most malware programs. It executed its buffer-overflowing payload against UDP port 1434 regardless of whether the target was running Microsoft SQL. Since most computers were not running Microsoft SQL, you might think it would be very inefficient. Nope. In 10 minutes, it changed the world by infecting millions of vulnerable computers in a speed record that still stands to this day. No malware program has ever come close to infecting as many hosts in as short of a time.

Data-Driven Defenses Focus on Initial Penetration Prevention

Without the initial penetration foothold, there really is no hack or hacker. If you want to stop malicious hacking, your defense needs to focus on preventing the initial penetration and the most popular, successful penetration methods against your environment, in particular.

How hackers break in has remained mostly unchanged for decades. The software and targets may change, but the general penetration methods do not. Unpatched software was being buffer overflowed in the 1970s, and it is still being buffer overflowed today. Computer worms and Trojans showed up in the same timeframe and are still very popular today. Social engineering has always been a top factor in successful computer maliciousness.

If you want a successful data-driven defense, you need to figure out which of the penetration methods discussed earlier in the "Initial Foothold Penetration" section are the most successful (i.e. damaging) in your environment. Today, the vast majority of companies will say social engineering and unpatched software are their two biggest problems, and if you don't have any local evidence to the contrary, you should focus on minimizing those penetration methods first. One day in the future these methods may no longer be considered the top reasons for successful exploitation, and any computer defense needs to understand that changing reality.

The Top Exploit Methods Change Over Time

Today, unpatched software and social engineering are the biggest threats for most organizations and have been so for a long time, but that wasn't always the case. Back when I started in computers in the 1980s, boot viruses (on both Apple and DOS computers) were the biggest security problems. Before that, the few computer worms and Trojans in existence ran mostly on mainframes and mid-range computers. When IBM PCs and DOS became popular, so too did malware and hackers on those platforms. Then Microsoft Windows became the dominate platform, and Windows malware took over. How the malware ended up exploiting a system or network was often unpatched software and social engineering.

In the 1990s and the first decade of this century, the biggest malware threats were macro viruses and malicious email attachments, which eventually morphed into email with embedded links carrying toxic payloads. After 2010, most malicious compromises have been due to websites exploiting unpatched software or social engineering via email. Now, Android malware is pretty popular, and the world's security experts are anticipating that hackers and malware will increasingly focus on the Internet of Things (IoT) platforms.

The most successful and popular attack methods have changed over time, as illustrated below, and will always continue to change. Any computer security defense needs to plan for this and strive for early and faster trend detection.

The general timeline of the most popular malware threats from the 1980s to 2017.

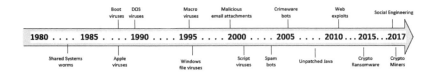

The most popular types of malware change over time, as shown above. What is the most popular type of malware program or attack type today is not likely to be the same in 10 years.

Overall penetration hacking methods don't change as much or as rapidly as malware program types, but they, too, change over time. Although unpatched software and social engineering remain the two most popular hacking methods, by far, their percentages of popularity have ebbed and changed over the years.

Over a decade ago, unpatched software was the number one hacking method. Social engineering was number two. Now, their popularity has switched. Today, social engineering accounts for 70–90% of all malicious data breaches and unpatched software around 20–40% (they are often exploited in concert together). Other hacking methods go up and down in popularity, and one day some other method may kick social engineering and unpatched software out of their hacking dominance.

Even when the overall hacking penetration methods maintain their popularity for an extended period of time, the way they are accomplished changes and evolves. For example, for almost two decades, the most abused unpatched software was related to the Microsoft Windows operating systems. After Microsoft built in default automatic patching, attackers started to focus on even more ubiquitous and more unpatched Internet browser add-in programs, regardless of the underlying operating system.

On the malware scene, for a decade, Internet browser pop-up screens falsely claiming to have found computer virus infections on computers (aka fake antivirus) ruled the world. Today, Trojans coming across social media sites and pushing ransomware programs are a bigger threat. As the popular saying goes, "Nothing ever stays the same except for change."

There are many reasons why the most popular exploits change over time. Sometimes the underlying technology that the exploit requires is no longer popular (e.g. floppy disks are needed for boot viruses, etc.). More often, the totality of all the needed defensive mitigations finally successfully addressed the underlying root cause of those exploits to the point that the threat was minimized.

An example of the latter point is macro viruses of the mid-1990s. As macro viruses became more than a nuisance, vendors began preventing untrusted macros from executing by default. Within a few years after those changes, macro viruses went from the number one problem to just a low-level nuisance that mainly infected the unpatched and the easily socially-engineered (although macro viruses still occasionally enjoy short periods of greater popularity).

Attackers will move on to more successful exploits as the ones they were using become less successful. A data-driven defense takes this into account and does not overly fixate on a particular threat past its peak risk window. Instead, it strives to detect new and rising exploit trends earlier. A proper data-driven defense is a living, responsive framework that works the same regardless of the types of threats. When properly done, it will help you prioritize the top risks and shorten the exploit-response cycle for each of them.

The Exploit-Response Cycle

It's hard to convince everyone involved to protect against threats and exploits that do not yet seem to exist or aren't causing a lot of pain. It can be done, but in general, it's far easier to sell defenses against a demonstrated, existing threat causing lots of damage. It's just human nature.

Many times, we cannot predict what a future threat or exploit will be or how bad the damage can be until it occurs. Even if we are aware of a potential new threat, it's hard to prioritize the risk if it hasn't yet occurred "in the wild" or isn't occurring in significant numbers.

Additionally, most emerging threats and exploits have a lengthy "shelf life" from when they first appear to when they become a serious, overwhelming problem. The longer time scales of most exploits sometimes take years, making the appropriate response that much more difficult to determine.

People are great at dealing with the biggest, most immediate pain in their lives (like a bee sting), but they are not so good at recognizing slowly emerging trends in their early stages, when they are more of an annoyance than a huge threat. This is how mosquito-borne malaria has killed billions of people around the world and still kills over a half million people each year.

Most of the time, the scary but far less likely threat wins in a battle for people's priorities. Mosquitos kill more people in a single day than all the shark attacks in the last hundred years (https://www.gatesnotes.com/Health/Mosquito-Week-2018), but you don't see the Discovery Channel running a series called *Mosquito Week*.

As long as threats aren't too painful or immediate, people don't pay them all that much attention. Similarly, fires, bombs, tornados, and earthquakes get a lot of attention. Climate change over decades? Not so much.

People who control the budgetary purse strings are hesitant to spend money on a threat that has not yet revealed itself to be a big problem. It is the reactive "cat-and-mouse" nature of our responses to nearly every threat, which almost ensures that most threats and exploits are allowed to grow in occurrence before we finally respond in an adequate way.

People respond to newly emerging computer security threats in the same way. In my experience, it takes most companies (and vendors) one to three years to adequately respond to an emerging threat. A good computer defense plan recognizes that most exploits have a bell-curve-shaped, extended lifecycle and attempts to shorten the timeline of critical, emerging threats.

Regardless of the responsiveness of our defense, most emerging threats undergo a similar *exploit-response* cycle as shown in the following figure.

The exploit-response cycle

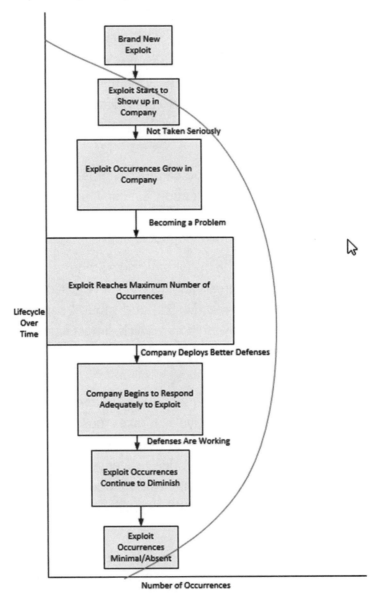

All computer threats and security defenses undergo a similar
cycle of response and remediation with each individual exploit.

Even though the most popular exploits change over time, the bell-curved exploit-response cycle does not.

Early on, the company may not be prepared at all to deal with an emerging threat. If the company is not experiencing exploits from the new attack vector, it may even feel cautiously optimistic that it won't experience the attack. Often by the time the company realizes that the new attack has made a significant negative impact, the exploit is widespread and out of control.

If the exploit continues to spread, the company must eventually respond to it if it wants to survive, and it must change or increase remediation methods to handle the exploit. Over time, most companies begin to get a handle on the exploitation method, decreasing the number of successful exploits.

Eventually, either due to the company's remediation responses or technology changes, the exploitation method ceases to be a top threat. Historically, the time between the early and mature stages of computer defense has often taken longer than it should as compared to a strategy that uses data to document growing threats.

Of course, in the real world, there are multiple, overlapping exploit-response cycles, one for each different type of exploit, each in its own stage of maturity. And hackers can change their exploit vector far more quickly than we can respond, leaving defenders in an always lagging lifecycle. Computer security defense is challenging!

A Data-Driven Computer Defense recognizes the defense cycle stages and attempts to more quickly identify growing, emerging threats and implement appropriate mitigations to lessen risk sooner. We will explore this more in later chapters.

Why Hackers Hack

Although all hackers use the same methods, different types of hackers target your organization for a variety of motivations.

Just a decade or two ago, all we had to worry about was teenagers writing mischievous computer viruses that displayed messages like "legalize marijuana" or played digital tunes like "Yankee Doodle Dandy" or individual criminals looking for bank accounts. Those impish "script kiddies" and solitary malicious hackers have been replaced by organized crime gangs, corporate hackers, and nation-state-sponsored hacking groups. Oh, how I pine for the playful hackers of yesterday. Let's take a closer look at the main types of hackers based on their motivations.

Nation-State-Sponsored

Any country worth its salt now has teams of nation-state-sponsored cyberwarriors. The largest countries have tens of thousands of professional hackers. Many hackers work for their military, looking for digital edges to help their country maintain an advantage in both the real and digital world. Cyberwarriors often look for and steal military-related intellectual property and projects. They spy on individuals and companies. They also assess their enemies' cyberdefenses, looking for ways to disable critical functionality if their country ever needs those types of services.

Corporate Espionage

Many professional groups around the world look for and steal valuable corporate secrets, regardless of whether they have military value. They often steal information from competitors. They may do so patriotically for their country, mimicking the official nation-state-sponsored hackers discussed in the previous section, but they don't have official state sponsorship or a purely military objective. For example, they may steal corporate intellectual property so another company in their country can be more competitive. They may steal internal cost details to help another company negotiate a better position or steal an attorney's case file and offer it up, for a price, to the opposing lawyer. The key differentiator is that corporate espionage is usually more about financial or corporate motivations than purely nation-state objectives.

The lines between nation-state-sponsored hackers and corporation espionage can often be very thin. For example, the 2014 hack against Sony Pictures by North Korea (https://en.wikipedia.org/wiki/Sony_Pictures_hack) is one of the most damaging attacks in history. Apparently, the sole motivation for the hack was to punish Sony financially and reputationally for the future release of a comedic movie portraying North Korean leader Kim Jong-un in an unfavorable light. The hackers accessed and publicly released hundreds of gigabytes of Sony's internal information, including very valuable intellectual property and embarrassing internal emails.

Financial Crime

A large percentage of hacking occurs solely to financially enrich the hackers in one way or another. This category contains any hacker or malware program that exists solely to steal money or other financial instruments. It includes ransomware, financial information theft, bank account stealing Trojans, ATM skimmers, credit card number theft, phishers, spammers, buyer scams, Nigerian emails, e-currency theft, stock manipulation programs, data hostage programs, and other programs or schemes that look to move value from the victim to the aggressor. In the corporate world, it often appears as either fraudulent banking transactions and money transfers or fraudulently ordered products and services. If money is the motivation, it falls in this category.

Hacktivists

Hacktivists are hackers primarily motivated by an ideology, be it political, environmental, religious, moral, or otherwise. They are out to spread their philosophy and harm others who do not share their same belief system. They can do this in a variety of ways, including denial-of-service outages, public information campaigns, doxing (releasing potentially harmful information about a particular target publicly), embarrassment, and public misinformation campaigns. As long as it results in negative press or a financial loss for their target, they've accomplished their job.

Adware

Adware is malware that maliciously modifies your computer to promote a particular product or service. It can do this in a number of ways, although it usually does so by intercepting your Internet search engine queries and either displaying pop-up ads or redirecting you to a web page that you would not have been directed to by a normal search engine query.

For example, say that you type in "man of steel promos" in your favorite search engine because you want to find video clips from the latest Superman movie. Instead of being directed by your default search engine to the best movie clips, your browser is directed to mobile phone Pokémon games.

Stolen Resources

Many hackers break into computers to use the computers' resources (e.g. CPU, memory, electricity, storage space) for free. Decades ago, this category was mostly used by hackers who stole digital movies and music and used other people's large hard drives to store the content for free. Today, this category is mostly represented by hackers looking to gather large pools of electricity and CPUs to help "mine" (i.e. generate) new cryptocurrencies. Mining new cryptocurrencies, like bitcoin, can cost the miner more in electricity and other resources than what they gain with the resulting newly generated cryptocurrency. Hence, if they can "borrow" the "leftover or unused" resources, they can create cryptocurrencies on someone else's dime. This is a form of financial theft.

Gamer Theft

These types of hackers are a special sub-category of financial criminals, but they are so numerous and aggressive that they deserve their own section here. They are comprised of individuals who want to have unfair advantages in a particular game or service or cause operational disruption. Often, they create malware that searches for computers that are participating in a single game (or series of games under a single publisher). The malware then steals the victim's authentication information or maybe just game credits. Game credits can be used to purchase items in the virtual world or be resold at a discount for another type of currency. Hackers may also use DDoS and ransomware techniques to harm other gamers and services, either to benefit monetarily or to gain a competitive advantage in the games.

Information Brokers

This group of hackers gathers private data and sells it to other interested parties. The information could be valuable databases, legal case information, passwords, or customer lists. Information brokers differ from corporate espionage hackers in that they are more interested in obtaining immediate financial reimbursement for the stolen information than in the intellectual property aspect of it.

Botnet Makers

Another large group of hackers includes those who simply want to compromise your PC or device with a *bot* so that it becomes a node on one of their *botnets*. The botnets can be rented, by the hour, to whoever wants them. They can be used to steal information, compromise companies, take money, or participate in distributed denial of service (DDoS) attacks. In any given moment, literally millions of PCs and devices on the Internet are part of someone's botnet.

Insider Threat

In most big companies, there are one or more employees who do not have the employer's best interests at heart. They can be industrial spies, but they often fall under the financial theft category or, occasionally, the nation-state-sponsored category. Insiders often target a company's credit card or customer databases, hoping to supplement their income. Many steal corporate secrets and offer them to competitors. Sometimes they steal customer lists on their way out the door. A few each year are even brazen enough to cause operational harm.

Traditional and Other Types of Hackers

Do not discount the traditional hackers, who are hacking for their own individual needs, be it financial gain or just to prove they can do it. Years ago, traditional hackers conducted almost all of the hacking. Most were content to just write a computer virus that printed a funny saying on the computer or played a prank at a predetermined time. However, a few of these hacks even caused real damage, like the Michelangelo boot virus did when it formatted hard drives. But most were just someone's vanity project, a way of saying that the hacker was smart enough to do it but didn't want to cause real, widespread harm. Unfortunately, today this type of traditional hacker is less prevalent. Now talented hackers often roam in groups or corporations with an intent to inflict real damage.

Although the motivations discussed in this chapter cover the majority of all malicious hacking, there are endless possibilities, and you have to defend against all of them.

The Importance of Understanding Hacker Methodology and Motivation

Grasping a hacker's motivation helps you understand their ultimate objectives and what value they hope to obtain from your company. That's very important, especially when creating your threat scenarios for risk evaluation.

For example, if your company is frequently compromised by bitcoin miner malware programs, it probably means your company's intellectual property isn't the primary goal of those hackers (unless it's a ruse to hide their true intent). The potential damage calculation is limited to stolen CPU cycles and electricity. The damage from corporate espionage or nation-states can be far higher than "borrowed" computer resources.

You have to understand the motivations of the main hacker groups that are attempting to break into your company to be able to more accurately calculate potential damages in risk assessments. A data-driven defense values hacker methodology, particularly the initial root penetration exploit, more than other defense frameworks. If you want to stop future acts, understanding how something breaks in is as important, if not more important, than what the hacker did once they were in. A data-driven defense soldier recognizes that learning how "pesky" adware got into an environment can be as important as how some uber-password-stealing backdoor program got in, because both might have used the same initial penetration technique. Stopping nearly harmless adware just might be the key to stopping the bigger and more dangerous threat. This topic is discussed further in future chapters.

Chapter 2 summarized hacker methodology and motivation, which is key to defending against them. Chapter 3, "Broken Defenses", discusses what is wrong with most traditional computer security defenses.

3 Broken Defenses

Why are most of today's corporate computer security defenses so wrong? Obviously, no company, leader, or IT security employee wants to defend inefficiently or against the wrong threats. Everyone wants to put the right defenses in the right places against the right things. So, how did most corporate computer security defense plans get it so wrong? Chapter 3 explains this.

> "*If you protect your paperclips and diamonds with equal vigor, you'll soon have more paper clips and fewer diamonds.*"—Dean Rusk, US Secretary of State, 1961–1969

Risk Misalignment Is the Central Problem

Computer security defense has always been about identifying threats, determining vulnerabilities, ranking risks, and then applying mitigations to minimize those risks. Unfortunately, the complexity of numerous computer security threats and their constantly evolving nature has led many defenders to respond too slowly or to focus on the wrong threats. This misalignment has resulted in enterprise defenders often failing to:

- Identify in a clear and timely way all the significant localized threat scenarios they face

- Focus on how initial compromises happen (i.e. root cause)

- Understand the comparative relative risks of different threats

Chapter 3

- Broadly communicate threats ranked by risk to all stakeholders

- Efficiently coordinate agreed-upon responses (i.e. mitigations) to risk

- Measure the success of deployed defensive resources against the threats they were defined to mitigate

All these implementation weaknesses lead to a misalignment of computer security defenses against the highest risk threats.

The Evolution of a Data-Driven Defense

Starting nearly two decades ago, I saw the same key problems of risk and defense misalignment at each company I consulted with. Simply put, companies were not ranking the various risks correctly. Each company was not focusing on and fixing the right things even when I explicitly and correctly outlined the top risks that they faced.

At first, I wondered if it was an issue with the way I was delivering my security reviews. Was I, despite my own self-image as a good communicator, a poor communicator? Was I the problem? I started to make sure all my security report findings were ranked by criticality, from the top threat to the weakest, and I said so in the text and tables listing the various threats and remediations. I put the top threats in a thick, red, bold font.

Ranking threats against each other and telling the customer what they should be focusing on first isn't super common in the computer security world. Security consultants and their companies are hesitant to empirically rank one threat above another because they are afraid that if one of the lower ranked threats later becomes a bigger problem for the client than a higher ranked risk (and this does happen), the client might then disparage or even sue them because they feel they had been directed to focus on the wrong issues.

For that reason, most computer security consultants either simply list all problems without ranking them or broadly classify them as being high-, medium-, or low-risk. In most computer security reports, the safest thing for any consultant or company to do is to list most or all of the threats as high-risk. That way if a particular exploit happens in the future, the consultant had told the customer that the risk was high, and it's the customer's fault that they did not listen and fix it immediately. For the consultant (or defense tool), there is less risk in ranking everything as high-risk.

But I decided to take a professional risk and hope my employers, who at the time absolutely agreed with the other less decisive consultants, wouldn't find out. Emotionally, it would have been less stressful for me to feign ignorance, let my customers keep prioritizing the wrong things, and apologize after the fact. But if I took that safer route, I felt that I would be a fraud and not doing the best I could for my customers. I didn't want to be part of the reason that they stayed at risk and continued to be successfully compromised.

Instead, I took a professional risk with both my employer and my customers. I actually looked at the data that showed how the company was currently being successfully compromised and would most likely be compromised in the future. I ranked those vulnerabilities and risks the highest. In most reports, only one, two, or maybe three things got most of the risk. Everything else was ranked as having far less of a chance of leading to a future successful compromise.

My recommended areas to focus on could have been wrong. I could have been ending my career early. Instead, two things happened.

First, my prioritizations were almost always right for predicting their biggest future problems. Every now and then—really just four times in two decades—the problems I predicted as their top threats didn't turn out to be how they were worst hacked the next time out. Sometimes the next successful hacker simply tried something else that wasn't historically a big problem in that company. My ranking method, which early on was mostly based on my gut feeling and experience, wasn't perfect, but it was accurate enough that it encouraged me to keep pushing to make it better. Eventually, I figured out that the customer's own data and experiences were needed to increase my method's accuracy.

Nevertheless, I could never have predicted the second thing that occurred. Even though I could fairly accurately predict how they would get hacked the worst the next time, rarely did a company follow my prioritized recommendations, even in the face of my previous successes. In fact, most of the time it seemed like they were excited to have me there, paid a lot of money to get me and the report, and absolutely agreed with my prioritized findings. And then, with only a few exceptions, most companies focused on everything except for what I had recommended. I was dumbfounded, over and over.

I started obsessing about the reasons behind this result. I interviewed hundreds of people, customers, and other security consultants (who all had similar experiences), and I kept a keen eye open for the underlying causes. I never missed a chance to ask a customer or consultant about why what was supposed to be the top priority was never treated like the top priority. The most common answers are captured in this chapter.

I've been describing data-driven defense concepts to private clients and writing about it since at least 2007, although they didn't coalesce into a unified theory with the *data-driven defense* moniker until my first public whitepaper on the subject in 2015 (http://aka.ms/datadrivendefense).

Common Examples of Misalignment
Here are some common examples of misalignment that I saw at many companies.

Unpatched Software
From 2007 to 2015, the most common way businesses were hacked into was through unpatched software, and in particular, unpatched Oracle Java™. In fact, , in their *Cisco 2014 Annual Security Report* (https://www.cisco.com/assets/global/UK/pdfs/executive_securi ty/sc-01_casr2014_cte_liq_en.pdf), Cisco indicated that unpatched Java was responsible for 91% of all successful web attacks.

Imagine that! Patching a single program would erase the vast majority of most corporations' computer security risk. And trying to fix anything else that was web-related, all together, would not equal 10% of the risk.

And yet, during that same period of time, most corporations had large percentages of unpatched Java. In the same report, Cisco said 76% of their customers were running a Java version that couldn't be patched (e.g. end-of-life and unsupported). I had been seeing similar circumstances for years with my own customers. It's not a coincidence that the most unpatched Internet browser program was also the most abused. That's why hackers exploited it. I would tell company after company to focus on patching Java. It would absolutely be the number one reason for cybersecurity damage to their environment, year after year. And yet, year after year, it remained unpatched and badly abused.

I got so frustrated with the lack of attention being paid to it that I would start loud, somewhat unprofessional, rants while reading out my security review findings, saying that this single problem was their biggest problem and almost nothing else mattered if they didn't fix it. I felt that if I went a little overboard when describing what they needed to fix that they would remember it and be more likely to fix it.

If they complained that senior management wouldn't let them fix the problem because it might cause service interruption (which is a huge, realistic fear in the IT security industry), I would reply with something similar to this: "Suppose I told your CEO or the company's board of directors that I found the number one problem with your IT security and that if that one problem was solved it would immediately eradicate 90% of the risk, and that everything else, all together, didn't equal 10%, and that I told you this, and you didn't fix it? If the CEO and board of directors knew this and didn't take steps to immediately fix it, how do you think shareholders would feel about their leadership? How would your customers feel about the data you store about them?" It was a veiled warning to get their attention. I was desperate. They would nod their heads in agreement that unpatched Java had to be fixed as the top priority and ask me how to do it.

And on my next visit, unpatched Java was as bad as ever. Every time without fail. They would tell me how they were putting in multi-factor authentication, smartcards, and new servers and getting rid of the weak LANManager (LM) authentication protocol—essentially doing everything but patching Java better.

One customer, who had over a million instances of unpatched Java, told me they had removed Java from their weekly patching and vulnerability reports because that data point so skewed the other items that the reports' charts didn't look right. They said that everyone already knew that unpatched Java was the biggest problem, so they removed it from the report so that other things could also be focused on. I kid you not! This is a public company, which had lost over a hundred million customer records, had been fined hundreds of millions of dollars, and had dozens of outstanding lawsuits related to the last successful big hack. And even then, I could not get them to focus on the right things. Unfortunately, their lack of focus is not unique. It was the same at nearly every company that I consulted with for a decade.

Most companies aren't confident enough to claim they do good patching. They know they don't. But there are always a few companies who claim they have very good patching and have it under control. It is never true. In my professional career I've never scanned a single system or device that was fully patched—not one router, workstation, server, or appliance. They were always missing something.

Fortunately, you don't have to accomplish perfect patching to get most of the benefits. Most hackers abuse the most popular programs, which usually are Internet browser-related, email, or word processing programs. Out of the tens of thousands of programs you might need to patch, maybe 5 to 10 programs have the majority of the risk. I would consider a company that perfectly patches these 10 programs as superior.

Most companies think they do great patching because some patching report says they are 95–99% fully patched. That is a decent overall patching level. I know CSOs who would kill to have those high levels of patching compliance.

But what an overall patching rate doesn't reveal is the patch success rate of the most likely to be abused programs, which is the most important figure in calculating risk. The patch success rate against the majority of programs that aren't likely to be attacked doesn't matter nearly as much. It's the patching status of the mostly likely to be abused program that determines whether a company is at an elevated risk of successful attacks due to software vulnerabilities.

For example, say the company patches all of its programs except for Java. That's one program out of hundreds that may be installed on most computers. One out of a hundred gives you a 99% patch compliance rate. That sounds great until you marry it up with the fact that 91% of all successful web compromises involve unpatched Java. The overall patch compliance rate means very little when compared to how perfectly you patch the most abused programs. Your real potential risk for exploitation is probably closer to 91%, not 1%.

Unfortunately, because the focus on patching is misdirected in most organizations, the structural incentives behind most patch management programs are wrong. In most enterprises, patch management is left to one or two employees who are rewarded based on their overall patching rate (or perhaps their patching rate for lower risk operating system patches), rather than how well they patch the highest risk programs. Indeed, patch management employees are often prevented from patching the very programs that they themselves know would provide the most protection. Despite the continued presence of high-risk attacks, most companies still tolerate large percentages of unpatched Internet-related software for various, and often substantial, operational reasons. These include that critical applications may break if the software is patched and a lack of real authority is given to the employees charged with patching software. It is well accepted in the computer security industry that it's easier to get fired by causing a substantial operational interruption than it is by deciding to accept residual risk by leaving high-risk programs unpatched. Hackers love the irony.

It's also very important, with your new and growing data-driven defense mindset, to understand that the most unpatched program in your environment may not be your biggest risk. During the same time period discussed above, 2007–2015, the most unpatched program in the world was Microsoft's Visual C++ redistributable program, which is often included with third-party applications. More PCs had unpatched versions of it than even unpatched Java. The key difference was that the Microsoft program was never located in a standard place and was rarely running as part of an exploitable service, both of which made it much harder to exploit than Java. Hence, Java was the much bigger problem. Even though unpatched Microsoft Visual C++ redistributable was almost never patched, it was never exploited once "in the wild" as far as I know. Real risk is about more than simple numeric counts.

Repeat after me: "There is a huge gulf of difference between all the biggest POTENTIAL threats that the world is telling you about and your biggest damaging current and future mostly likely SUCCESSFUL threats." There is a huge difference between what you're being told to worry about and what you should be worrying about.

I'm going to repeat this as a mantra throughout this book. Understanding the difference and how to apply it correctly in a defense makes you more valuable in your job.

Social Engineering Threats

As I write this (in 2019), the number one security threat at most companies is social engineering. Unpatched Java eventually fell in importance because OS and browser vendors finally responded with multiple ways to diminish the risk, including not installing Java or not allowing it to run within a browser.

Since then, social engineering has moved up as the number one threat in most organizations. I'm not sure if it accounts for 91% of all successful attacks in most companies (as Java did for a while), but it easily accounts for the most successful break-ins in most companies and is absolutely involved in most of the largest and most damaging attacks. The surveys and data I'm seeing put it at 70–90% of all successful malicious data breaches. No matter what the actual number is, it's the number one problem by far and has been that way for many years now.

So how much anti–social-engineering training do most employees receive each year from their corporations? According to multiple surveys, most companies give less than 30 minutes per year to the topic! Most organizations spend less than 5% of their IT security budget directly addressing the biggest successful risk in their environment. That's a huge misalignment. Perhaps companies don't need to spend 70–90% of their budget on fighting social engineering, but it should probably be more than 5%.

There is nothing better that most companies could do right now to decrease their overall computer security risk than to provide more and better anti–social-engineering training. They can create it in-house or buy it as a service from a multitude of very competitive companies. This would likely cost less than most of their other IT security expenses (such as antivirus software, firewalls, intrusion detection systems, etc.) and yet be the single most important thing they do. Better patching of specific programs is likely the number two problem.

Unless defenders can demonstrate that their environments are less susceptible to these risks than those of their peers, it seems reasonable to conclude that most companies should work harder to decrease the potential success of social engineering attempts and significantly improve patching, particularly of the most exploited programs, as their primary defense strategies.

In a data-driven computer defense, the fact that social engineering and unpatched software are the biggest threats would be confirmed against the enterprise's actual experience, backed by data. If confirmed, this would be communicated to all stakeholders, including senior management. Senior management would assign the necessary resources—and give them the authority—to combat the top threats. A special task force project team might be created to look at the overall problems, discuss mitigations, do testing, and reduce the risk posed by social engineering and unpatched programs. If every stakeholder understood the large threat posed by social engineering and a few unpatched programs, it's doubtful that they would stand by and do nothing (or still continue to give end-user education and patching such a minor focus). What a data-driven defense is asking IT security to do is to focus more on the left flank of the battle when the adversary is currently being more successful.

How Did Defenses Get So Misaligned?

Misalignment of mitigations against the biggest threats they are supposed to address isn't the root cause of broken defenses. It's an unfortunate response to multiple underlying competitive pressures, which if properly dealt with would get rid of the inefficiencies. It isn't natural for an army or a company to ignore responding appropriately to their biggest risks. So how did things get this way?

There are a number of reasons, including lack of focus—competition for attention, lack of accountability, slower budgeting cycles, inefficient IT organization, human evolution, flawed threat intelligence, lack of focus on root causes, too many high priorities, poor ranking of threats, inadequate detection capabilities and metrics, and poor communications of top threats. I explain each in more detail in the following sections.

Lack of Focus—Competition for Attention

The sheer number of threats plus an astonishing array of other factors compete for the attention of computer security defenders and management. Here are some common factors that cause a lack of focus on the right threats:

- Sheer Number of Threats
- News Cycle's Threat of the Week
- Compliance Concerns
- Too Many Projects
- Higher Priority Pet Projects/Politics

Most experienced IT security practitioners will likely agree with those reasons listed above and be able to list even more causes for the lack of focus within their environment. IT environments are complex with multiple stakeholders, each with their own concerns and recommendations.

The Sheer Number of Threats

In the computer world, a considerable variety of new threats arrive like water from a fire hose. The military analogy that started off this book would better reflect the reality of a company's digital environment if it showed the good army being attacked over and over by every other bad army in the world, without a break, with a brand-new enemy army joining in every 75 minutes. I truly believe that IT security professionals have the toughest job in the world.

As the figure below from CVE Details in February 2019, (https://www.cvedetails.com/browse-by-date.php) shows, there are between 5,000–16,000 new vulnerabilities reported each year (or about 13–45 per day, day after day). That's a lot of threats for defenders to understand and evaluate.

Annual reported vulnerabilities from CVEDetails.com as of April 10, 2019.

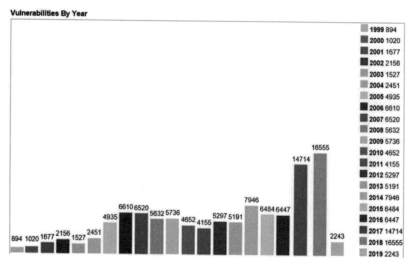

Each newly discovered vulnerability is cumulative, adding to the previous numbers, never going away until the underlying technology goes away. It's not like defenders only have to worry about the 5,000–16,000 new vulnerabilities that are going to threaten them this year. They have to worry about the 5,000–16,000 threats from last year, and the 5,000–15,000 threats from each of the previous five years, and so on. There are probably 100,000 software vulnerabilities that defenders must be aware of and fight against in a given year.

Defenders are well aware that a large percentage, usually between 30–40%, of all vulnerabilities are ranked with the highest criticalities (see the following figure taken from https://www.cvedetails.com/cvss-score-distribution.php on April 10, 2019 as an example). Vulnerabilities with CVSS Scores 7 and above are considered to have the highest criticalities. CVSS Score calculation and rankings are defined here: https://www.first.org/cvss/specification-document.

Criticality of vulnerabilities by CVSS Score

Distribution of all vulnerabilities by CVSS Scores

CVSS Score	Number Of Vulnerabilities	Percentage
0-1	1092	1.00
1-2	863	0.80
2-3	4453	3.90
3-4	3912	3.40
4-5	24586	21.70
5-6	21936	19.30
6-7	15337	13.50
7-8	25567	22.50
8-9	503	0.40
9-10	15273	13.50
Total	113522	

High (7-8) and Critical (9-10) CVSS criticality scores essentially means that the vulnerability, if successfully exploited, could completely control the computer, if not the entire network the computer is on. Whenever anyone runs a vulnerability assessment report on their network, it always includes dozens to hundreds of pages of high-risk vulnerabilities. How do you know what to fix first?

A large percentage of the exploits are "low complexity", which means easy for a hacker to take advantage of (see the following figure, also taken from the "Microsoft Security Intelligence Report, volume 21").

Complexity of vulnerabilities

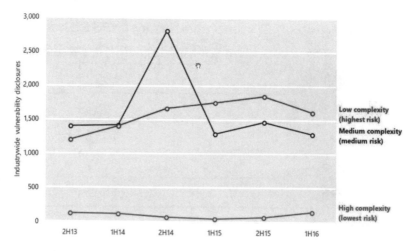

So, defenders are being told to worry about 5,000–16,000 vulnerabilities, year-after year, many of which have the highest criticality and are easy for the hacker to exploit.

And that's just brand-new, unique vulnerabilities. It doesn't include the fact that malicious hackers have tens of thousands of old vulnerabilities to exploit and have generated tens of millions of pieces of unique malware. Not only do defenders have to worry about nearly every threat ever found (because old threats rarely go away), but they must address every new exploitation vector that the bad guys create.

To further complicate matters, defenders are often in charge of simultaneously protecting multiple OS platforms (Microsoft, Apple, Linux, Android, and iOS, for example), multiple form factors (PCs, slates, a variety of mobile devices, IoT, wireless, etc.), and multiple types of networks (wireless networks, local networks, wide area networks, Internet, and cloud threats).

Defending against a particular type of attack, or even the same malicious threat, often requires different defensive techniques.

The end result is an incredibly large and growing number of new and old priorities competing for limited resources, without the time to give each potential vulnerability the consideration it deserves. The sheer volume of things a computer security defender must be educated on and worry about is overwhelming by any description. It is a very challenging environment.

The News Cycle's Threat of the Week

Many times, despite your best intentions to focus on the right things, your agenda gets hijacked by the latest news cycle. Every IT security employee knows the dread of hearing about the latest "big" exploit on the television or from online media while getting ready for work in the morning. Even if your organization isn't susceptible to the latest big threat, you have to spend time and resources to rule out the vulnerability and assure senior management that you and your team have it covered.

It doesn't help that all the security vendors trying to sell you products and services super-hype up every newly found vulnerability, even if the announcement comes on the same day that a patch is available or if it requires that your end users bypass four warning prompts to execute. Security vendors' primary selling tool is fear, and they try to talk up the dangers of the new threat as best as they can. Security vendors love naming their newly found exploits after dangerous creatures (i.e. "the lion virus" or the "Satan worm") and even give them trademarked or open-source cartoon characters, a la sandworm

(https://sensorstechforum.com/the-sandworm-malware-how-
dangerous-is-it/).

*Example of the SandWorm Trojan cartoon character designed to
help generate more publicity of the vulnerability*

I don't blame the security vendors too much for their sales
hyperbole. It's their job, and it's easier to sell batteries in
hurricane season. Everyone's got to make a living and the
threats are real. Most just oversell the risk. My pet peeves are
when they over-promise defenses or suck money away from
better projects. That latter issue is even more of a problem with
defenders than salespeople, and this book will teach you how
to avoid that pitfall.

Compliance Concerns
CEOs and other senior management officers are legally
responsible for their company's security, and the way they
comply with this is by attesting that their company meets the
many required compliance laws and regulations. Although this
has always been implied, over the last decade it has been
codified in multiple laws passed in many countries.

CEOs not meeting compliance requirements can be fired or
otherwise held responsible by their board of directors,
shareholders, governments, and the court system. Companies
not meeting compliance requirements can be subject to hefty
fines and kicked out of large customer markets.

In the CEO's world, compliance equates to job security. Hence, if an IT security worker needs to get something done sooner rather than later, they need only tell senior management that it's critically needed for compliance before the next audit. "Compliance" is the magic word to make any IT need an instant top priority.

There are two problems with this. One, compliance requirements often take precedence over security, and two, real security and compliance are often at odds. For instance, as mentioned in Chapter 1, the new recommended password policies are better for a company's security risk, but every existing regulation and guideline requires that you meet the old ones. So even though the password ilovellamasverymuch is an incredibly strong password, it will be rejected by most regulatory requirements because it doesn't include enough character sets (e.g. uppercase letters, numbers, symbols, etc.). But they will happily accept Tuesday2, which is far weaker and easier to hack, as acceptable. Sadly, you can be assured that a significant portion of your security efforts will be subverted to satisfying compliance requirements, real security be damned!

Too Many Projects

The average company for which I conduct security reviews has more than 50 simultaneous IT security projects, with dozens of "top" priorities. Because of the competition for scarce resources, most of these projects will never be completed. Those that do get completed will most often be implemented poorly or neglected soon after implementation. Most projects will drag on forever, go over budget and over schedule, then get de-prioritized, and eventually be dropped. Even worse, rarely do the top projects that are actually completed lead to significantly better security against the right threats in the right amounts in the right places.

Many IT security workers and project managers, faced with too many competing "number one" projects, will ask management to reprioritize their rankings. They will plead "Tell me which number one priority is my real number one?", only to be told that they are all number ones or that they have three number ones. If they are lucky enough to get a true ordered list, often their newly anointed number one will be moved lower down on the list in a few weeks by a new ad hoc project that no one planned on. I'm sure most of my readers are nodding their head in agreement on this claim.

If a company wants to impress me, they need only complete one or two serious projects per year that directly focus on their biggest threats and do them well. I've rarely seen this actually happen in my career. Do less to do more.

Higher Priority Pet Projects/Politics

Another big problem occurs when senior management comes up with a new, ad hoc, pet project that they give a higher priority to and has to be done "ASAP". Budget constraints that hindered every other project are suddenly loosened for the new project. Money allocated to other long-argued and officially approved projects is reallocated to the new project. The best team members on other projects are "borrowed" for the new project, which also demoralizes everyone who was working hard on those projects.

Every senior executive comes up with their own pet projects that they feel the company really needs to have, even if they don't have the data to back it up. Sometimes they just finished a trendy new management book, attended a single seminar touting the new product, or heard about a new idea on the radio on the way to work. Or even worse, they have become friends with a particular vendor or enjoy the perks that come with doing business with a particular vendor (e.g. travel, sports events, golf junkets, concert tickets, etc.). It's unethical and sometimes explicitly illegal, but that doesn't stop it from happening. Often, the product or service you're being forced to implement isn't as good as the competitors', but the senior executive assures you that they have an inside channel to the product team and can get everything fixed. You just need to install it now.

All of these reasons end up creating an avalanche of growing unranked and misranked threats and projects. But there are problems beyond sheer numbers alone, including the additional reasons described in the following sections.

Lack of Accountability

Most IT security projects do not deliver the value promised, and the vendor and the corporate sponsor often are not held accountable. Many vendors come in promising the world, such as "we can detect all malware" or "there are no false-positives", and then they get the deal and come up with a million reasons why the buyer's incorrect implementation is the only reason the product didn't live up to the hype.

I was once on a conference call with a very well-known security vendor selling an appliance that was being promoted as the answer to their customer's advanced persistent threat (APT) problems. The vendor was asked if they could detect APT, and the vendor assured the potential customer that they could. I then asked the vendor to take us step-by-step through how they were going to detect APT using the details of what the

APT last did to the customer. I wanted to know how the APT was detected, since the attacker used a zero-day exploit to capture a local admin password that they then used to act as the legitimate user across the network, doing things that the legitimate user could do. I asked them how their product was going to tell the difference between the legitimate user doing their usual job and the APT using that same user's credentials to do whatever it wanted to do. Granted, there are many ways to do this, depending on how the product works, but in this case, the appliance being touted didn't have those sorts of capabilities. You could have heard a pin drop in the room. The vendor was silent for an uncomfortably long period of time before saying that they would need to do some research and get back to us, which they never did. I saved that customer millions of dollars that day.

Another time a vendor touted their product's ability to get any security answer that anyone could need from all of the customer's computers in less than one minute. They provided more than one hundred predefined sample queries, which when tested, worked quite well at delivering the predefined answers. I then asked all the computer security people in the room what questions, if they knew the answer to, would significantly help them in their job. In a few minutes we came up with 12 questions, such as "How long does it take our antivirus software to detect all the malware that it eventually detects?" and "How many computers in the environment have a digital certificate signed with the SHA1 hash algorithm instead of SHA2?" (because SHA1 at that time was soon to be decommissioned) The vendor's product could not answer any of their questions. The vendor hemmed and hawed and said that if we or they wrote customized scripts that their product could then run, then we could get our answers. It showed the product didn't do nearly as well once you strayed from the vendor's predefined queries.

If more vendors were held accountable for their promises, there would be less worthless junk out there.

Slower Budgeting Cycles

IT budgets are set in a minimum of one-year cycles, and big projects often take multiple years to get reviewed and approved. Hackers can change their attack methodology in seconds. Because defenders are always REACTING to threats, the inherent nature of slower budgeting cycles means IT can rarely meet a newly emerging threat head on as it occurs. It often takes companies a year or longer to respond to a serious emerging threat.

Inefficient IT Organization

Generally speaking, the larger the organization is, the more layers of built-in bureaucratic inefficiency there are. For one very large company, I was hired to create a new "high-security" baseline for their servers, which I was told was going to be deployed on "all" of their servers. After months of work and testing, I found out that "all" meant only the servers under this particular division's control. And this division had the authority for just 11% of the organization's servers.

Although I was confident that our new baseline would significantly reduce risk in this organization, we could not even get the majority of the leaders to meet with us to consider the new baseline, much less have or get the authority to enforce it. Many organizations are like the Tower of Babel, with a multitude of separate business units that can't communicate or work with each other. It makes it extremely hard to push a good idea.

Corporate Culture Risk Tolerance

I ask every company I do a security review for what their risk tolerance is for malicious hacking. They always say "low" or "zero", implying that they take computer security very seriously. But the truth is that most companies actually have very high levels of computer security risk and don't take them as seriously as they think they do.

A company taking computer security risks "very seriously" locks down the computers under their management with a very high degree of control. They do not let users have local administrator credentials, they only allow preapproved programs to run (e.g. whitelisting), and they disable the Internet, among other things.

This sort of control, especially disabling the Internet, is unpalatable to most corporations. But if you don't disable the Internet or at least limit employee access to a small number of predefined sites, you're essentially saying that you choose to embrace the highest risk computer activity there is while only concentrating on things that collectively will not matter as much. I get it. Employees would quit or never join your company in the first place if you significantly limited their Internet activities. But it also means your organization truly doesn't rank computer security that high as a priority. It's a common, normal outcome when you consider security and end-user usability at the same time.

Outside of some high-security military organizations or some very small business units within corporations, I've never seen computers as locked down as I have just described. The reality is that most companies tolerate a lot of security risk in most areas and only require lower risk in a few. Nearly every company is like this, and what they consider to be high- or low-risk depends on the corporate culture, scenario, and defined expectations.

Another example is that many companies prevent regular end-users from being local administrators (which is good) but still allow them to install any software program that will work under that constraint. Many high-risk Internet browsers and applications will gladly install and operate in a regular, non-privileged user's security context. It's not quite as bad as allowing a browser to install in an administrative context, but it's still allowing regular users to install the highest risk programs at their whim. A company's overall culture of risk tolerance has a huge impact on the ranking of their threats and projects.

Human Evolution

Human beings are biologically bad at ranking any risk beyond an immediate life-threatening danger (e.g. gunshot, knife attacker, etc.), even when we have the data and know the odds.

For example, I live in Key Largo, Florida, and I frequently take visitors out on my boat to swim, dive, and snorkel in the warm, azure waters. Nearly every visitor asks me if there are sharks in the water. They have usually seen the movie *Jaws* or the Discovery Channel's *Shark Week*. I always reply "yes" and add that although every saltwater ocean contains sharks, there has never been an unprovoked shark attack in Key Largo in recorded history (since the late 1800s). I tell them the odds of a shark attack in a given year are 1 in 3.7 million (per ocean dip) throughout the world, but it is apparently much rarer in Key Largo.

I then ask them how they liked the drive down high-speed, two-lane, U.S. 1 to the Florida Keys. They usually say it was fine or beautiful. I then tell them that the odds of dying U.S. 1 are thousands of times more likely than a shark attack and that they have already survived that much higher risk event so they shouldn't worry about the far less risky shark attack. They don't care. They keep a lookout for sharks the entire time.

On a similar note, many people, including myself, flying on commercial airlines are worried about dying in an airplane crash, even though the odds of dying in a commercial airline crash are 1 in 9.2 to 11 million, far less risky than the much higher risk car ride (1 in 4,000 to 8,000 in a given year) to the airport. In fact, the odds of dying in a car crash during your lifetime are a startlingly high 1 in 50, while the odds of dying in a commercial airline crash during your lifetime, even if you are a frequent flier, are 1 in 20,000. You are 400 times more likely to die in the car, but people don't care. We are more scared of plane crashes. We know such fears are irrational, and yet we have them anyway.

The longer the timeframe for the potential threat is, the less likely people are going to care. This explains many people's failure to adequately care about global climate change or our disappearing coral reefs.

The same problems with human evolution allow us to make similarly bad risk judgements when it comes to computer security. We often fear and defend against the "scarier", less likely risks far more often than the more frequently occurring, less scary things that we see on a regular basis. Or we forget about the high-risk thing that has been present for years in our environment to the extent that its real importance gets lost. Sometimes we fear computer security threats that have near zero risk.

A great example is the sale of anti-RFID wallets. The anti-RFID apparel industry has become a billion-dollar industry over the last 10 years, despite the fact that there has not been a single documented case of a real-life RFID contactless credit card crime being prevented by a shielding product. Yet, many of those same people who purchase RFID wallets don't have a problem clicking on any unexpected links in email that ask them to confirm their logon credentials.

Some of the best discussions on this subject of irrational risk ranking have been written by the world-renowned computer security expert Bruce Schneier (https://www.schneier.com), particularly in his book *Beyond Fear: Thinking Sensibly About Security in an Uncertain World* (https://www.schneier.com/books/beyond_fear/). If you want to know the real reasons why computer security is so tough to accomplish, read any of Bruce's books. I have every one of them in my personal library.

Flawed Threat Intelligence

Most companies' threat intelligence (TI) is incredibly flawed, especially when it comes to focusing on the threats that are most likely to impact their organizations both today and in the near future. Most threat intelligence departments are great at buying multiple TI "feeds" that report on global statistics and create end-user education reports that discuss exotic, extraordinary threat scenarios that have impacted a few people in the world.

As a rule, threat intelligence departments are not so good at telling their own organizations what their biggest successful threats have been and will be. Threat intelligence is so bad in most companies that I call it "threat unintelligence". Most companies' TI has many critical flaws, including:

- Lack of good, actionable data

- Failure to focus enough on actual, locally experienced attacks (vs. focusing on mostly externalities)

- Inadequate detection

- Little or no forensic analysis

- Failure to capture root causes

- Overlapping detection in many areas while critical gaps remain in others

- Inability to effectively communicate detections up the chain of command and to the entire organization

A key weakness in most companies' computer defenses is the lack of an adequate feed of good data on their own local threats and risks from which to drive the defense plan and mitigations. If you don't know what your actual threats and risks are, how can you effectively plan a defense?

Lack of Focus on Root Causes

If you want to stop hackers and malware, you have to stop the initial penetration exploits they used to break in and get their initial foothold (as discussed in the previous chapter). Hackers and malware can break in ten or so different ways, and it is far easier to focus on and fight that finite number of root causes (e.g. social engineering, unpatched software, misconfiguration, etc.) than to fight the millions of resulting, reliant threats one at a time.

For example, if a company patches all software in a timely manner, it stops every hacker and malware program that relies on unpatched software from beginning its exploit. A company likely only needs to focus on doing a better job of patching fewer than a dozen programs to get most of the benefit. Patch a dozen things and stop 10 million malware programs. That sounds pretty good to me.

How a hacker or malware program breaks in isn't always known, but most of the time it can be deduced. Many hackers and malware programs only break in using a single or a few particular methods (also known as *attack* or *exploit vectors*), and many others leave enough forensic evidence that investigators can often figure out how they did it.

> # Do you know the number one root cause of how your company is successfully exploited the most?

An even bigger problem is that people often focus on the wrong things even when the root cause is known. For example, starting about a decade ago, pass-the-hash (PtH) attacks became very popular in Windows Active Directory environments. In a PtH attack, the hacker usually steals a local administrator's credentials and uses those to get the credentials for a domain admin, which then gets them every Windows password hash in Active Directory. And if passwords are shared with other systems, then the entire environment can be owned! Before vendors had better defenses, PtH attacks were a huge concern to most enterprise customers, and they are still a top concern today.

But what I tell customers is that the real problem is not PtH attacks. It's that an attacker got local administrator or domain administrator credentials, and if they have that, they can do anything. A local administrator can do anything on the local computer that is possible with software or hardware. A domain admin can do almost anything to an Active Directory network, including modifying the operating system code enough so that they can hide from anti-malware tools and forensic investigators. Even if you somehow prevent all PtH attacks but still allow the attacker to become an admin, you've not lowered your real risk at all. The hackers can still do anything else they want. PtH attacks are but one attack type out of millions.

Worrying about PtH attacks and not figuring out how to stop attackers from getting admin access in the first place is like worrying about your car's brakes when the thieves have stolen the whole car. In the computer security world, if you don't stop the root causes, you'll never stop hackers and malware. And most companies do a very poor job of tracking root causes and creating related actionable data.

Too Many High Priorities
One of the key difficulties in appropriately ranking threats is assessing their criticality (i.e. how much damage they can do if successful). A perfect IT security risk manager is supposed to determine the odds of a particular threat successfully occurring and then guess how much damage could possibly occur. But since there are millions and millions of threats, and that number is only growing all the time, risk managers cannot adequately and appropriately rank each threat.

What most IT security employees and managers do is take the threat intelligence's documented criticality ranking for each exploit and treat it as their real risk. Nearly every newly announced vulnerability is given a criticality ranking by the vendor or an analyst. The problem is that a large percentage of vulnerabilities are ranked with the highest criticality. There is very little relativity to other threats or to a specific organization's real risk.

So, although this approach reduces the overall number of threats someone theoretically needs to be worried about from 5,000–15,000 each year to only one-third to one-fourth of that number, that's still multiple thousands of new vulnerabilities that a typical IT security employee has to process and rank each year.

What ends up happening is that all the highest criticality threats get classified as "highly critical", with one no more important than another. There are occasionally exploits that get an especially high "above highest" criticality rating because it's been aggressively detonated "in the wild", has become "weaponized" (in a fast traveling computer worm), or can exploit a very popular piece of software; but even those "highest of the high" get lost in the avalanche of rapidly growing numbers in a short period of time. What you end up with is an amalgam of "top priorities" where no single exploit is treated higher than another or some threats become misranked higher or lower than they should be.

Poor Ranking of Threats

All of these problems described in the previous sections, especially the sheer number of threats, many with the same high criticality ranking, day-after-day, overwhelm defenders.

Instead of being able to rationally and empirically rank each incoming threat, they end up either misranking them or unintentionally ranking too many of them equally in a growing accumulation of threats whose importance they don't really understand. Because security defenders are besieged by so many threats and have neither the time nor the resources to accurately analyze comparative risk, they see them as illustrated below (like bubbles in a glass of champagne), not as relative to the actual risk of each threat to the organization.

In most traditional computer security defenses, threats are not ranked correctly and do not focus on root causes.

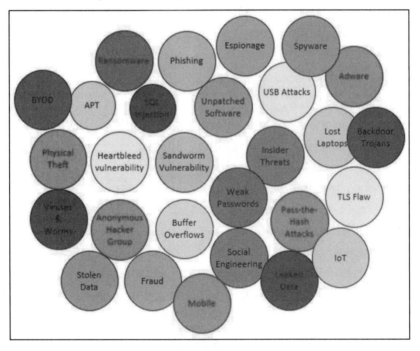

Without a focused set of threats ranked by the localized risk to an organization, it's easy to see why the defenses that are mounted would mirror the misranked threats in an absurd game of "whack-a-mole", which is very inefficient and doomed to failure.

In traditional computer defenses, every mitigation is treated somewhat equally

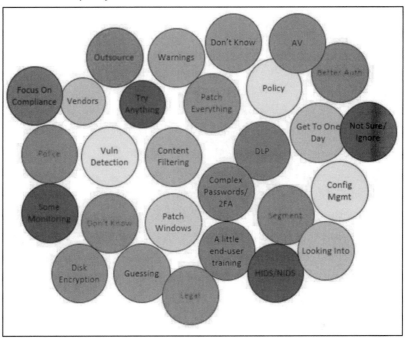

Worse, and far more common in most environments, is that the mitigations that are given the greatest resources do not align to the risks with the greatest potential impact/damage. This not only is an inefficient allocation of resources but also results in larger threats continuing to remain more impactful (i.e. Assume Breach).

In a data-driven defense plan, risks are effectively ranked against each other by using local data and focusing on root causes. In most companies, a handful of root causes/threats account for the vast majority of the organization's risk.

Example of root cause threats ranked by actual risk to the organization—the larger the circle, the greater the risk/impact of the threat

Example of root cause threats ranked by actual risk to the organization—the larger the circle, the greater the risk/impact of the threat

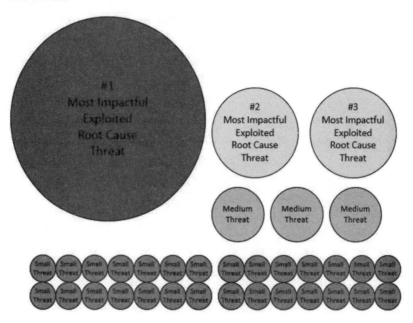

If IT defenders had a clearer picture of the relative organizational risk of each threat or exploit, they could better align their defenses to that risk and focus on root causes.

Example of defenses ranked according to how much risk/impact the threat poses to the organization—the larger the circle, the more important the defense

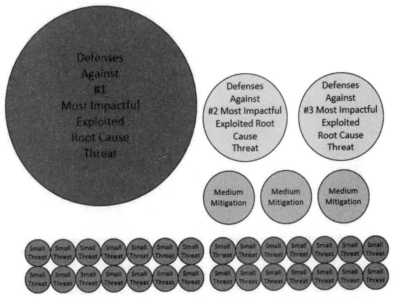

May decide that the cost of defending against small threats is not a good business decision

Inadequate Detection Capabilities and Metrics

In general, most companies do not do a good job of detecting localized current and emerging threats. It's not that most IT environments don't have the ability to detect these threats; it's that they often focus on the wrong things and don't understand the gaps.

Understanding how a company was compromised (i.e. root cause) and how long the compromise went undetected is far more important to a defense plan than names and numbers alone. For example, most companies can generate a list of all the malware families that their anti-malware software detected and removed. They can present actual numbers and identify the specific malware programs that were removed. But if they cannot tell you how that same malware was introduced into the environment in the first place—such as through social engineering, unpatched software, or a compromised website or USB drive—or say how long the malware program was in the environment before it was detected, then all those names and numbers are of less interest to me.

Poor Communication of Top Threats

Most large organizations do a poor job of communicating the biggest threats throughout the enterprise. At every company I consult, I ask the IT security department employees, individually, to name the top threats, in order, that successfully compromise their company. Throughout my career, I've yet to find a single IT security department team that even comes close to agreeing upon the top threats. Usually, I get a fair number of even responses for each choice across team members, including what could be the correct choice. But often the correct choice can't be ultimately confirmed because there is no data to back up the real answer.

If the IT security department doesn't know what the top threats are, how can they effectively respond to them? How can the rest of the organization work together to address the top threats if the IT security department can't tell them what those threats are?

> Can your employees accurately describe the top root cause threats to your organization, in order?

I often ask CSOs what their top threats are. Sometimes they are ready for that question and quickly answer it or hand me a chart or report showing the top threats. The CSO's top threats NEVER correlate to exploitation root causes or say something like social engineering or unpatched Java. Instead, their report usually says something like "Cloud Threats", "Insider Threats", etc., even when those threats are currently zero while the real successful threats are happening in the millions.

I get it. The CSO is expected to think long term and is thinking about the grand scale of emerging threats. That's their job. But if the CSO doesn't understand that RIGHT NOW the biggest number of successful hacks is tracked to a single unpatched program or a particular social engineering technique, how are you ever going to get the right resources in the right places?

Many front-line IT security employees and managers blame senior management for their failures to concentrate on the right projects, but if senior management doesn't have a clearly communicated picture of the top threats, ranked in order, how are you ever going to get the right support in the right places? In a lot of companies, it is the mid-level managers who are unknowingly keeping both the field-level employees and senior management in the dark about the top problems. This is never done intentionally. They are just doing the best they can while being asked to do a Herculean job of balancing too many projects with not enough resources. They are trying their best to deliver the best outcomes.

But if no one knows what the real top problems are, that sets in motion a situation that looks a lot like the army battle I described in Chapter 1. This leads to an inefficient allocation of resources, focus, and accountability to the wrong threats and defenses. Most companies' defenses look like my mythical, inefficient army. But it doesn't have to be that way.

Ask Yourself These Key Questions About the Biggest Threat to Your Environment:

1. Can your IT security team give the right answer?
2. Is the answer consistent across team members?
3. Can senior management give the correct answer?
4. Do you have data to back up the right answer?

If not, then you're ready for a better Data-Driven Computer Defense.

Chapter 3 explored all the reasons why traditional IT computer security defense plans misalign mitigations against the wrong threats. Chapter 4, "Fixing Broken Defenses", discusses how to fix all the wrongs and make them right.

4 Fixing Broken Defenses

The first three chapters described how most corporate IT computer security defenses are broken and why. Chapter 4 begins describing how to create a better defense plan.

> *"Never doubt that a small group of thoughtful, committed citizens can change the world; indeed, it's the only thing that ever has."*—Margaret Mead

To recap the biggest problem from the previous chapters: How are most traditional computer defense plans broken? Answer: There is a substantial misalignment between the biggest/most damaging actual threats and the applied mitigations.

The central problem with most computer security defenses is a misalignment between the biggest/most damaging successful threats and applied mitigations.

In most cases, defenders don't adequately understand what the most damaging successful threats really are, so it's hard to focus on fixing the right things in the right order with the appropriate effort. This creates a misalignment between the most important threats and applied defenses.

We fix it by focusing on the right threats and applying mitigations in the right amounts against those threats, and we determine how to do this by using better data to support our actions. That's a Data-Driven Computer Defense plan in a nutshell. This is the whole reason this book exists: to help readers better apply the right defenses in the right amounts against the right things in order to most efficiently lower computer security risk.

What Is a Data-Driven Computer Defense?

A Data-Driven Computer Defense is a methodology and framework that helps allocate security resources to more efficiently mitigate the top IT security threats. If applied correctly, it more efficiently minimizes initial breaches and resultant hacker and malware activities. It does this by focusing on objectives that:

- Improve data collection and analysis
- Collect better threat intelligence
- Improve threat detection
- Focus on root causes
- Improve enterprise communication and coordination
- Better align mitigations to the most critical threats
- Increase accountability

The following sections examine each of these concepts in more detail.

Improve Data Collection and Analysis

Most traditional computer security defenses are ranked more by gut feelings and project attention than data. A data-driven defense appreciates the importance of experience and intuition but supports conclusions and defensive mitigations with collected data. Data should drive as much of the plan and resulting process as possible and push aside gut feelings and unsupported intuition when they conflict with the data.

A Data-Driven Computer Defense (or more simply written, a data-driven defense) uses the scientific method, which has been used to advance science and society for hundreds of years. The insurance industry only survives because of actuaries who can fairly accurately predict current and future risk events. Science and the scientific method of using collected data to back up conclusions drives every industry. It's just very weakly correlated in the computer security world at this point in time. The computer security world can only benefit by collecting and analyzing more accurate causation data, just like every other industry.

There are many ways to gather and use data in a data-driven defense, but at the bare minimum you want to start by answering the following question:

What are the top SUCCESSFUL, most damaging, current and future most likely root cause threats, in order, to my environment?

You can't begin to efficiently fight the top threats if you don't understand and communicate what they really are. Of course, the "top" threats don't usually directly correlate to a simple numbers-counting game where the most abundantly appearing threat always wins. Top threats should be defined as "the most damaging" to the organization in a given period of time. One big damaging event could be worth more than a million other less damaging events. For example, a single stolen intellectual property incident due to social engineering could be far more costly to an organization than a million appropriately detected and deleted malware programs.

You need to evaluate your existing environment to document what data you currently have. Then do gap analysis. Most threats should be measured by damage or potential damage, if known, not just by occurrence numbers. Do you need to buy or create new data sources to better support your new data-driven defense systems? What are the gaps? What are the biggest gaps? What just needs to be improved to be better? What are the redundant systems, and can some of them be removed?

Every computer security leader needs to evaluate what information they have today on their current and mostly likely future threats, determine the gaps, and then figure out how to improve. Understand that there can be a gulf between the biggest potential threats and the threats most likely to be successful against your organization. There are usually huge gaps between potential and actual successful threats. The winners understand the difference and try to focus on preventing the most likely SUCCESSFUL threats, backed by data. As a part of that process, most companies usually need to improve automated data collection, identify growing current and future issues, and prioritize remediations.

Data-Driven Security Gap Analysis

One of the key actions of any data-driven defense is to figure out where you have gaps in:

- Threat intelligence
- Threat detection
- Mitigations

You need to take inventory of the current state of your organization in each of these three areas, document how each matches up with the others, and identify where the gaps are.

You begin by figuring how well your existing threat intelligence aligns with your organization's current and most likely future successful threats. In my experience, usually the gaps here are huge, with companies spending hundreds of thousands of dollars on threat information that does not apply all that closely to their own experience. So, the question to ask is "What cyber maliciousness is occurring to our organization and how well is it being documented or predicted by our current threat intelligence?" Document the gaps and figure out what is needed to close them.

Then take inventory of every event, log, and alert that could possibly detect maliciousness (as defined and supported by better threat intelligence), in your environment. Make a list of every bit of possible threat detection data source, including inputs, intent, what existing databases they get saved to, if any, how they are used, who has access, who actually uses them, and what the outputs are. This is usually a huge undertaking in most environments and often results in many dozens to over a hundred threat detection sources being logged and discussed. It commonly includes dozens to many dozens of existing threat detection databases.

Then compare all the threat detection data sources to the most likely current and future threats. To facilitate discussions, I usually summarize everything on a single spreadsheet, listing all the threat data sources on one axis and all the current and likely threats on the other.

Now conduct a group discussion to identify all the places where current threat detection could detect the most likely threats. You'll usually have many areas where a single type of threat would be detected by multiple threat detection sources, and you'll also have a bunch of gaps, where no existing detection source would adequately detect the likely threat. You may want to rate threat detection coverage on a scale from 1 to 5 or something like that. Threat detection doesn't always provide a yes-or-no, black-or-white answer. Sometimes threat detection exists but needs to be improved.

The resulting analysis will be used to figure out what is needed to fill in the gaps. You'll also use the data to make sure you don't allocate unnecessary resources for threat detection in the areas that are already well covered. You may even decide to drop redundant coverage areas.

Next, having identified your top threats and detection abilities, make another matrix spreadsheet with the top threats on one axis and the implemented mitigations on the other. Then examine for gaps. Again, just as with threat detections, you want to use the data to make sure you don't allocate unnecessary resources for threat detection in the areas that are already well covered. You also want to discuss what you need to buy or create to cover the gaps.

Every proposed future project should be examined against the results of this gap analysis to show how well it supports or doesn't support current gaps. With a data-driven defense, you'll likely see someone's "pet number one project" get ranked with less urgency after examining the data. As long as someone isn't intentionally "lying with statistics" to overly promote or hurt a proposal, using data to drive project priorities is what you want to happen.

Periodic "rhythm-of-the-business" gap analysis is a huge part of a Data-Driven Computer Defense. Defenders should continually be assessing and reassessing incoming SUCCESSFUL and MOST

LIKELY threats against existing threat intelligence, threat
detection, and mitigations. If you're doing it right, gaps should
be continually identified and reduced. The figure below
graphically summarizes the data-driven gap reduction cycle.

The data-driven computer defense gap analysis reduction cycle

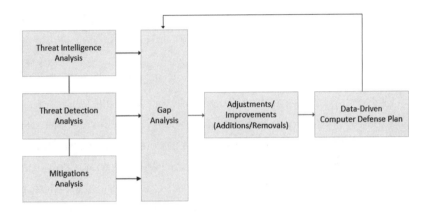

Of course, you don't have to use spreadsheets or comparative
matrixes to accomplish gap analysis. All IT defenders should
have already been performing gap analysis, and it can be done
many different ways using a variety of tools. The important
thing is that routine gap analysis is done on threats, detection,
and mitigations, using good data instead of gut feelings.

Some readers may be expecting me to tell them exactly which
data sources they need. Later in this book, I reveal in more
detail many pieces of data that I think all companies would
benefit by knowing, such as "biggest successful threats" and
"mean-time-to-detection. I'll also reveal additional common
pieces of data that I think all organizations should have. But the
right answer is that every computer security defender needs to
assess the strengths and weaknesses in their own situations.

If I or anyone else published the "only" data you should care about and everyone knew it and followed it, the bad guys and their malware would just change to avoid being tracked by that measurement in much the same way that polymorphic malware evades antivirus detection. The key lesson is to figure out what the right questions are to ask and how well you are currently answering them. See Chapter 6, "Asking the Right Questions", for more details on improving the data itself.

Collect Better Threat Intelligence

Assuming your organization has a threat intelligence role or team, I'm going to bet that it needs to be improved. Most collected threat intelligence is so unrelated to the organization collecting it that it tends to be more "noise" than useful data. It's often so bad that I call it "threat unintelligence". Most threat intelligence goes on and on about big, global threats, emerging threats, and even very unlikely to happen threat scenarios to the exclusion of the things that are actively happening to their own organization on a daily basis.

Perform this test: Ask your threat intelligence team to tell you the number one root cause reason why your company is most successfully attacked or damaged. The majority of the time, all you will get back is silence or "we are working on it" replies. You might get a guess, but rarely do you get a definitive answer backed by data.

This is ironic because the only reason for the existence of the threat intelligence team is to keep the organization, which is paying its bills, knowledgeable about the most likely current and future successful threats. Everything else doesn't really matter.

As Chapters 2 and 3 discussed, there are thousands of new threats released each year, on top of all the previous years of threats and hundreds of millions of malware programs. Threat intelligence should report on those that are currently the most successful and those emerging threats that are likely to become the future's most common successful threats.

To do this, the threat intelligence team should start with gaining intelligence about today's most successful threats against its organization. Nothing could help more than to know the current state of successful threats and why (i.e. root cause) they are the top problems right now. That should be followed up by the most likely SUCCESSFUL future threats, which is then followed up other local recent historical experiences, and then everything else.

As explained in Chapter 2, threats/risks have an exploitation lifecycle that follows a bell curve from a point of gaining traction to their peak and then an eventual descent.

Ranking Threats Against Each Other
A Data-Driven Computer Defense plan is interested in measuring each of the top threats causing the most damage over time and comparing them to each other—one curve for each threat/risk (see below).

Example of top threats by damage over time. Each line represents a particular threat type and/or root cause.

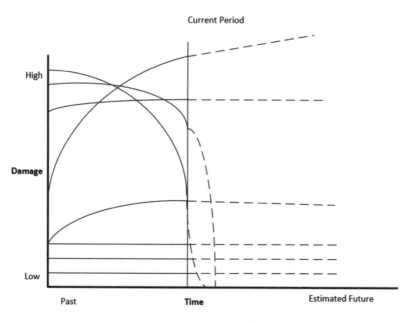

A data-driven defense plan is interested first in the top threats currently causing the most damage followed by those most likely to cause the most damage in the near future. The example figure above shows this for different threats, as measured against each other. This is a key understanding.

> Note: If you don't have this data today, I'll tell you how you can get it fairly easily in Chapter 9, "More Implementation Examples".

You should use the threats causing the most damage to help you directly identify which ones to be concerned about. But a data-driven mind is also interested in whether the damage from each particular threat is in an increasing or decreasing state over time. If it's still increasing (i.e. the damage this time period is more than it was the last time period), then current

100

mitigations are not sufficient and gap analysis needs to be performed. If the exploit/response cycle for a top threat/risk is decreasing, then perhaps the current mitigations are adequate. If the decrease is steep enough, perhaps additional mitigations don't need to be applied.

A similar chart that evaluates top threats by damage over time is shown below, but with letters to indicate the different threats.

Example of top threats by damage over time evaluated

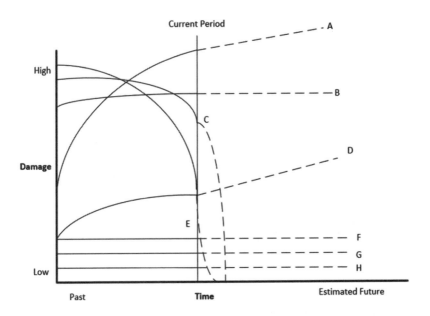

In this simplistic example, a handful of threats (A, B, and C) are causing far more damage than the rest. They are the current top threats that your theoretical company needs to focus the most on mitigating. However, C seems to be projecting downward and D seems to have an upward trajectory. Perhaps either now or if those trends continue to track identically over the next measuring period, you might add D as a top threat and downgrade C from being a top threat. The general idea is that you care about the top current damage sources and the most likely future top damage sources. It's up to the defenders to determine how much effort goes into mitigating the rest of the threats (E, F, G, and H).

Of course, in real life, threat cycles, like stock market gains, don't always go up or down in a continuous direction like the simplistic lines shown above. But like a longer-term investor, the data-driven defense mind is interested in the general trend. And if a current trend line turns against its previous direction too sharply or too often, then it needs to be investigated for the cause and mediated.

Local Successful Exploits Matter the Most

It is important to focus on the local SUCCESSFUL exploits your organization is currently experiencing the most. I don't just mean the uber critical hacking cases where a human adversary was involved in going after your crown jewels. I'm also talking about any malware that made it past your defenses without being immediately detected and deleted during its original download and execution. And I'm talking about successful social engineering of any kind. Successful exploits indicate gaps and weaknesses in your defense.

Not focusing on the organization's local successful exploits is easily the biggest flaw in most threat intelligence reports and why most computer security defenses end up misaligned. Most organizations give too much credence to national, global, and the most newsworthy threats while accepting or treating their own experiences as anecdotal or temporal, when it should always be the other way around.

Emerging Most Likely Threats

After the current top damaging threats are identified and mitigated, emerging threats that are successfully occurring to your organization should matter the most. Even in this category, you should care most about the emerging trends that are growing the fastest. Investors call this "alpha". Defenders should call it your most likely biggest future threats.

Upward trending threats are your "alpha". They usually reflect a confluence of changing hacker methods versus existing mitigation gaps. If you see a trending upward attack method that goes up, up, up over time, ask yourself why that is the case and what mitigation is missing.

Recent Historic Threats

The downward trends shouldn't be completely forgotten about. If a trend is consistently headed downward, then that usually means you have effectively deployed mitigations and have done your job. Just keep an eye on such trends to make sure they continue downward. If they suddenly lurch upward, there could be a new leak in the dike.

General Popular Threats

After documenting your own organization's biggest current and future most likely threats, it's finally time to consider the threats facing the world in general. Sometimes they hit you in the face because they impact some huge percentage of all computers in the world and a related threat is raging "in the wild". It's only a matter of time until your organization has to deal with it. Realistically, this falls into the previous category of emerging, most likely threats, except perhaps you only get a few hours to days to deal with it.

What I'm mostly referring to in this threat category is the general threats to a large percentage of computers that you haven't had to directly consider as one of your top organizational threats, at least yet. Even so, you should start with the general threats that seem to be abundant in your industry, competitors, or country before considering general global threats. The closer the threat is to your own organization and experience, the more you should care about it.

Focusing first on local successful exploit trends doesn't mean to neglect non-local reports all together. They do provide value. I remember when I was writing my first book in 1999, *Malicious Mobile Code: Virus Protection for Windows* (https://www.amazon.com/Malicious-Mobile-Code-Protection-Windows-ebook/dp/B071SHY9M9), one of my reviewers mentioned he was starting to see a lot of USB-infecting Trojan horse programs where he lived—South America.

Unfortunately, I actively discounted the upward trend that he was seeing because I didn't see the same thing in my own local experience—until it was too late and USB-infecting Trojans were everywhere, especially with the Conficker worm of 2008. Looking back at the data, the upward local trend was there all along. At first it was limited to a few foreign countries, but eventually it started to appear and increase in all countries. By the time Conficker hit the global stage, most people were not prepared, although my reviewer friend was. Conficker data-driven defense responses are discussed further in Chapter 9, "More Implementation Examples".

Another time that I ignored upward trends was when I was writing some whitepapers for a leading computer security vendor. I was writing about attacks and defenses that dealt with solid-state drives (SSDs). An officer in the company was a reviewer and he asked why I wasn't mentioning memory-resident-only, *fileless*, malware (i.e. doesn't save itself to non-volatile memory or storage like most malware programs).

Although I had seen some minor reports about it in the media and even in some other trusted reports, because I hadn't seen it personally, I blew it off. A year later, most of the biggest retail and financial sectors were attacked badly by memory-resident-only malware. Again, looking back at the emerging trends, it was clear that memory-resident-only malware was on the rise in a big way even if it didn't immediately impact the companies I was working for.

In the USB-infecting Trojan example, Conficker did eventually impact many of the companies I was working for. In the fileless malware example, none of the companies I was working for got hit in the next few years, but eventually fileless malware did become a major factor in most organizations. These days fileless malware is a common mainstream type of attack.

Emerging alphas, no matter where they originate from, local or global, should not be ignored. That said, what matters most by a longshot is how your organization is being successfully exploited today and in the near future. But I'm not saying to completely discount everything else.

Everything Else

Everything else falls into the lowest risk bucket. If your organization is normal, then most threats/risks fall here. The average organization has a few top threats, a larger number of near-top threats, and a bazillion threats/risks that all together don't account for a whole lot of risk.

Ranking Risk Using Threat Intelligence

It is impossible to prepare for all threats, and that shouldn't be the goal. Instead, defenders should focus on the most likely and impactful threats to their specific environment. To do that, each defender needs to create and gather threat intelligence from many sources, both inside and outside the company.

Start with your company's own localized experience, which in general is the most relevant and reliable. Your company will always be susceptible to other threats, but the recent history of successful exploitations against your company is one of your best data sources. Hackers and malware often will repeat attack methods that have worked successfully against your company in the past. The most successful attack methods are in direct response to an organization's long-term weaknesses.

After gathering internal data, including emerging threats, get additional data from partners and industry news, and then move out to external vendors and worldwide news feeds. As you move away from your company's own experience, the data will usually become less relevant. The figure below summarizes the general relevance of data sources as threat intelligence moves further away.

Threat intelligence relevance versus distance away from the company

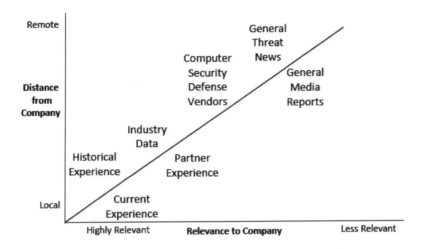

This is not to say that vendor or general threat information cannot have acute relevance during particular time periods. Common sense must prevail. For example, the first news of a fast-moving Internet threat often comes from external sources far away from the organization. But even in those instances, the threat may or may not be relevant to the organization depending on its existing defenses and platform makeup.

A Data-Driven Computer Defense focuses on local successful current, emerging, and historic attacks first, followed by the "in the wild" attacks most likely to occur to the enterprise or within their industry, followed by everything else.

Although an enterprise can be compromised by something new or rare (i.e. a zero-day), generally most of an enterprise's computer security risk occurs from existing, emerging, and historic local attacks. A Data-Driven Computer Defense accepts the risk that some unknown exploit may occur, but it actively chooses to focus on the known and most expected risks first. Because what else are you going to do, focus on remote and unlikely threats that aren't happening all that often to your environment?

It's also important to note that simply because a critical vulnerability in your organization is found once or thousands of times, that does not necessarily mean that the tested critical vulnerability translates into a real-life critical risk. A typical vulnerability scan in an average organization will reveal thousands of vulnerabilities, with a large percentage of them being ranked with the highest criticality. It's very normal.

> There is a gulf of difference between all the biggest threats/risks you are being told to worry about and the most likely successful threats/risks that you should worry about.

It's important to assess the likelihood and impact of those vulnerabilities being used successfully against the organization to access valuable resources. Similarly, a lesser-ranked vulnerability should be given higher criticality if it has been used in the past or is currently actively being used against the organization. Many times, an organization is "immune" to a particular global threat because of an existing mitigation (or set of mitigations). For example, maybe the organization has tons of software that contains weak SSH passwords, but they disable port 22 on all servers and across the network in a way that can't be easily circumvented (ex. IPSEC, etc.) or they require digital certificate authentication.

Conversely, you need to make sure you don't overly dismiss an existing or growing emerging threat that your organization might be susceptible to. All too many organizations think they must somehow be magically protected against a particular vulnerability because they haven't detected any related trouble. Don't prematurely declare yourself invulnerable to something if you're not adequately measuring or defending against it.

To repeat a point made throughout this book, criticality and risk are not something you should readily accept from someone else's data and pronouncements. Most external parties do not understand what defenses and mitigations are already deployed in your environment that will offset particular vulnerabilities, even if particular high-risk vulnerabilities do exist in your environment.

The concept of improved threat intelligence localization is brought into this book because most organizations neglect their own best data. By beginning with their own experience, data-driven organizations are most likely to be able to respond to the most likely SUCCESSFUL threat scenarios in most time periods.

Threat intelligence should be valued in the following order:

1. Top successful current, local, most damaging threats/risks/exploits
2. Top successful local emerging threats
3. Top successful historic threats
4. Top current non-local threats (e.g. peers, industry, nation, global)
5. Historic global threats most likely to impact you
6. Everything else

Take a look at your current threat intelligence and assess how well it produces and shares the most valuable, local experience data. Do a gap analysis. More than likely, some improvements will be needed. Often, an organization's threat intelligence is so broken that it cannot easily be refocused on local threats. It can take a lot of work, new tools, and new processes to pull it off. But if an organization doesn't have solidly ranked threat intelligence, their defense is closer to being the fool's army described in Chapter 1.

Improve Threat Detection

It goes without saying that you can't determine what your top threats are without accurately detecting them. Even the threat intelligence weaknesses I described in the previous section are held hostage to the people and processes that help determine the top threats.

For decades, most organizations didn't capture a lot of threat information. But after a decade of very damaging and highly publicized hacking events, if not localized experience, most organizations are capturing more information than ever. In fact, the opposite problem is true today. A single computer can generate hundreds of thousands of events each hour. One single domain controller might collect gigabytes of logs every hour and have to recycle them many times a day. Centralized log management systems collect hundreds of thousands to billions of events per hour.

Most organizations are capturing so much information that they don't know what to do with it. It's enormous. They spend a lot of money on devices, services, and hard drives. They are detecting more anomalous activity than ever, in fact, way too much. The information is often full of false-positives. It can quickly become overwhelming and unactionable.

Here's how to improve threat detection. First, inventory all event log sources. List everything that could possibly detect a hacker or malware. Second, define your threats. You may want to create threat scenarios to help you do this. Third, determine the most likely threats, including likely threat/attack scenarios. They can help with defining of needed threat detections. Fourth, analyze how well the most likely threats are detected with existing threat detection methods and tools, and then fix the gaps.

Developing Threat/Attack Scenarios

Creating threat/attack scenarios of the different ways a remote or inside attacker could compromise your environment can be helpful in determining threats and risks. For example, consider the following possible scenarios:

- An attacker launches a massive distributed denial of service (DDoS) attack against the biggest web sites.
- An attacker defaces your company's website.
- An attacker uses phishing to obtain company credentials.
- Hackers exploit unpatched software to give them remote access to end-user workstations.
- An attacker gives or sells a customer database to your competitors.
- An attacker uses password hash dumping tools to obtain all Active Directory credentials.
- A virus deletes random files on the main corporate network.
- An attacker obtains access to protected source code.

It is important to select risk scenarios that are most likely to occur and result in critical damage to your company. This is the point where most computer defense plans misalign defenses. Remember, there is a big digital gulf between discovered critical threats and the ones that are most likely to occur in your environment.

Start by documenting and using the scenarios that have most recently occurred, and then move out, much like the previously discussed threat intelligence data improvement suggestions, from scenarios that are more relevant to less relevant. Use attack scenarios to help calculate threat likelihoods and cost from damage.

Next, compare the most likely successful threats to the existing threat detections and figure out where the gaps are. A scale of 1 to 5 can be used to indicate relative strengths and weakness. Where critical threats exist with weak or no detections, create or buy new detection systems and make sure the new systems don't provide things you already have multiple redundancies for. For any new detection systems, make sure the systems and their vendors are held accountable for what they are supposed to deliver. It's easy for "sure fire" detections to end up causing so many false-positives that they become ignored. Threat detection indicators (more broadly known as *indicators of compromise* or *IOCs*) should be as accurate as possible. Some of the largest hacks in recent history have happened because someone incorrectly ignored the hacking indicator.

This doesn't mean that you can't implement and fine-tune an IOC later to make it more accurate. Just don't implement one into a production environment if it leads to a lot of false-positive noise and expect defenders to pay attention to the right indicators that indicate real maliciousness. IOCs for new threats often take teams of people to figure out how to minimize the false-positives and false-negatives.

For example, a few years ago, many of Microsoft's customers were getting frustrated by pass-the-hash (PtH) and related "golden ticket" attacks. In this instance, the golden ticket attacks occurred when attackers took over the Windows Kerberos authentication system to generate new, seemingly valid Kerberos authentication tickets to access any Kerberos system or service. See the Insider Threat Security Blog for more details: https://blog.stealthbits.com/complete-domain-compromise-with-golden-tickets/.

PtH attacks were and are very common. Golden ticket attacks were not as common, but both caused great concern for Microsoft's customers in 2014. Microsoft gathered dozens of subject-matter experts, including me, to figure out how we could create better detection and prevention mechanisms. I worked on one of the detection teams.

After testing the exploit over and over with common PtH attack tools, we identified several Windows log events that occurred consistently with PtH attacks and didn't seem to occur otherwise. Then we updated our threat detection software with these new IOCs.

Unfortunately, when we deployed them globally as a bigger test, we got a very high percentage of false-positives. We were able to figure out what the issue was and fix it, and now Microsoft's PtH and Golden Ticket detection IOCs are pretty rock solid.

Creating new threat detection methods is not always easy, and many entities outsource the detection to other third parties and make them expend the capital to develop the IOCs.

Bring Me 10 Perfect Detections

Most companies I consult with have a ton of false-positive detections, so much so that they either don't check the logs or don't respond to alerts. If your company is not responding to and checking out ALL critical alerts, something is wrong. Either you have the wrong events generating alerts or you have a slack response team. It's usually the former.

One suggestion I give most companies in this situation is to forget about trying to detect everything. List your top current threats and try to create an IOC that absolutely indicates that one of those top threats is occurring. Usually I give a random number, such as saying "Create me a total of 10 IOCs for the top three threats (10 in total, not 10 for each)". By refocusing everyone's effort on just a few threats, you're likely to get your top three exploits/risks detected if they were to occur, and your team will get used to the process. Once you have gotten your first 10, then move on to the rest. If you get 10 good security event detections, you're already doing better than most of the world. The rest is gravy. Creating good detection events is discussed in more detail in Chapter 7, "Getting Better Data".

Focus on Root Causes

Another missing element in most computer security defenses is a lack of appreciation for root causes. Understanding and diminishing root causes (e.g. initial foothold exploits, like social engineering, unpatched software, buffer overflow, password guessing, etc.) is the only way you will reduce risk over the long term. You can't stop future house burglars by concentrating on what the previous burglar stole after he was in. You have to concentrate on how the burglar got into the house in the first place if you want to prevent future burglaries from happening.

It is far more important to understand how malware or a hacker got into your organization in the first place than the hacker's or malware's name. Was it social engineering or unpatched software? If it was social engineering, what type of social engineering was it? Web-based, email, social media, or something else? If it was unpatched software, what was the most common unpatched software involved? If you don't focus on the root causes of a successful exploitation, you will never stop the exploitation. Further, the benefit of stopping a single root cause is that it also immediately kills all of the other threats/exploits that use it.

Here's an example: In the last few years, the *Unified Extensible Firmware Interface* (*UEFI*) replaced the more easily exploitable BIOS standard that governed PCs for decades. There are many UEFI (https://en.wikipedia.org/wiki/Unified_Extensible_Firmware_Interface) benefits, but the primary security one is that all firmware code is signed by the vendor and can only be updated by code signed by the vendor. Historically, a BIOS could be updated by any software, signed or not, and either modify your operations to bypass any security mechanism or make your device inoperable. For those of us interested in better securing firmware, UEFI was a godsend.

This is not to say that UEFI doesn't have its rightly skeptical critics. UEFI is also full of new code, so much so that it looks and runs much like an open-source Linux/Unix operating system. You can connect to the Internet (from the firmware), get to a command prompt, run scripts, and execute powerful programs. That was rarely possible with BIOS code. Additionally, UEFI contains enough common code and structure that potentially one vulnerability could impact all computers running UEFI at once. This is a big risk that UEFI developers understood and tried to address when making the new standard.

Although it is true that one vulnerability could impact all UEFI devices possibly more easily than it could impact all BIOS firmware devices, one UEFI fix prevents every known firmware exploit at once. In the BIOS world, you had to craft different fixes for each BIOS and version, and so you might have to craft literally—I'm not making this up—tens of thousands of different BIOS patches to guard against one type of exploit. But in the UEFI world, one patch can prevent every known type of exploit. In our future computing world, I'd rather have the latter type of solution than the former.

Another example involves the previously discussed PtH attacks. In order to successfully perform PtH attacks on Microsoft Windows, an attacker must be a local administrator (to retrieve password hashes off of a local Windows computer) or a member of the Domain Admins or Enterprise Admins groups (to retrieve password hashes off of a domain controller). Too many defenders focus on trying to specifically detect and stop a PtH attack, when stopping an attacker from getting privileged credentials is far more important. If you stop PtH attacks, you stop one type of attack. If you stop the bad guy or malware from getting privileged credentials, you stop millions and millions of possible attacks.

If you don't concentrate on reducing or eliminating the root causes of exploitations, you will never stop exploits! Refocusing on root causes needs to be communicated and goal-driven to all computer defenders. When they find a malware program, they should find out how it got there (e.g. social engineering or malware). If a hacker tool is discovered on a DC, someone needs to determine how it got there to begin with. If someone gets socially engineered out of their password, what type of social engineering was it? Are some types of social engineering more successful against your company than others? If unpatched software is involved, what are the most popular unpatched programs attacked in your organization and why? And so on.

How to Determine Root Causes

The top root causes (behind the top damaging exploit methods) should be determined. It's not always easy. Many times, new detection tools and procedures need to be created.

If you have zero data on root causes, consider surveying all exploited users. You can use an approach along these lines: "Hey, we found a malware program on your computer. You're not in trouble. We are wondering if you have any idea how the malware got on your system in the first place? If yes, was it A) someone tricked you on a web site, B) unpatched software, C) someone tricked you via email, D) web-based, E) other, or F) unknown." I've used this method before and some customers have chuckled at its rudimentary approach. Sometimes all you have is rudimentary, and rudimentary will often get you answers more quickly than waiting for a more expensive, better solution or no solution at all.

Sometimes the detected exploitation or location itself tells you the method and helps you identify the root cause. For example, most malware programs have hardcoded, distinct infection methods. An email worm may only work in email. A USB worm may only spread via USB keys. A stolen password may have been stolen using a phishing email. If you find a PtH attack tool on a DC that no one surfs the Internet from (which should always be the cause), then you can rule out web-based, email, and social engineering attacks from the DC itself. And so on.

Other times you can't easily determine root causes, although I'll give you some more ideas in Chapters 7, "Getting Better Data", and 9, "More Implementation Examples". But if you change your mindset to a data-driven mindset where the root cause is very important, not surprisingly, you'll start to learn more about and see patterns in root causes. Focusing on the root causes of exploitation is the only way to ever stop hackers and malware. Nothing else will work as well and efficiently.

Improve Enterprise Communication and Coordination

Once you understand the top successful root causes, communicate them to the rest of the organization. Explain what the top root causes are and how to avoid them. When everyone begins to focus more on root causes, they can begin to see how a "harmless" adware program is as dangerous as a password-stealing Trojan, if only because they both can use the same root exploit to get embedded in your organization.

Most IT security employees cannot answer this basic question correctly: What are the top SUCCESSFUL security threats to your organization, in order of damage? Even if they hazard a guess, they rarely have data to back it up. A Data-Driven Computer Defense plan answers that question using improved threat intelligence and improved threat detection. Once the top threats are known, they should be communicated throughout the organization.

This is done for several reasons. First, you can't begin to most efficiently fight something if everyone involved doesn't know what that top threat is. That's just common sense.

Second, it gives everyone a chance to respond to the threat in their own way. Their response can be personal (i.e. how they try to prevent the threat from personally impacting them) or focused on helping their business unit or the organization better respond to the threat.

Third, having everyone involved brings different perspectives, and it's more likely to tease out additional remediations, which could even be better than the original ones you thought of. History is replete with famous figures who at first appeared to be insignificant but then provided solutions that defended countries and changed the world.

Fourth and last, improving communication about top threats creates an organizational culture that teaches everyone to be aware of digital threats, how to rank them correctly, and how to respond. Involving everyone also educates them about the process of communications and mitigations around all computer security threats and will likely lead to faster responses to emerging threats.

There is no benefit to not communicating the top threats to everyone. That would be like knowing there is a burglar in your community and not warning everyone about what he is doing and how they can best try to stop him.

Create Cross-Boundary Communication Teams

The larger the organization is, the more likely it is to have organizational boundaries that tend to slow down effective communications. Create a cross-boundary communication team to better ensure that the entire organization knows the top threats and what you are doing about them.

Let me give you an example using my previous Microsoft work experience. For a long time, if a particular threat was reported to Microsoft, say malicious HTA files infecting users' desktops through Microsoft Internet Explorer, Microsoft did a good job of responding to that particular threat. But where Microsoft significantly improved over time was in looking at all the other ways that HTA files could infect a user's desktop. So, even if the initial vulnerability was directed at Internet Explorer, that team also got all the other product teams involved (for example, Outlook, SharePoint, Microsoft Office, etc.). Over time, Microsoft got better at finding similar issues in more products than were initially believed to be impacted. At first, it made Microsoft's overall vulnerability numbers go up, as one root cause could result in many different bugs to be found and fixed, but it ultimately reduced risk exposure for Microsoft and its customers, and it did so more quickly than if the organization waited for hackers to exploit them.

None of that would have happened without better communication about the top threats across the organization. Microsoft created a cross-business unit team that met at least once a week and held conference calls on newly emergency threats. Any critical new or growing threat was discussed, and anyone could ask questions of the subject matter experts. People on the call would then go back and discuss the threats with their own impacted teams and, if appropriate, bring those resulting discussion decisions back to the larger council. It has been one of the best data-driven defense ideas ever pushed at Microsoft.

Make Sure Every Employee Understands

With a Data-Driven Computer Defense, it is crucial that every employee understands the top threats. You want to be able to ask the key question "What are our top successful threats?" to any employee and get the same answer. Everyone from the CEO down to the janitor or food service employee should know the answer.

This is not to say that different employees don't have different levels of focus and need different details. I expect a CEO's understanding of the top threats and how they are being handled to be different than a regular IT employee's understanding of them, which will be different than a janitor's understanding of them. But all employees should be able to state what the top threats are. If not, that information is not being communicated effectively enough.

Focus, Focus, Focus

Focus is a huge part of a data-driven defense. Once you have identified your top threat, communication about it should be constant and consistent until it is no longer a top threat.

As an example, every piece of IT security literature that is used to educate employees should lead off with the top threat and how to prevent it, every single time. It should focus on the top threat until that threat is no longer the top threat and something else takes its place.

Instead, what I see in most employee IT security literature is communication about a lot of things, most of which are not the direct top threat to the organization. Even the best organizations may have only one or two pieces of education material about the top threat, and that's it. It's as if everyone involved thought that because the top threats were adequately covered once or twice, they've done the best they could and now they want to move on to other topics so they don't bore the reader. No!

With a data-driven defense, the top threats get covered constantly and consistently until they are no longer the top threats. It's okay to cover other threats in your education material, but every piece of employee education literature should BEGIN with covering the top threat and how to reduce it. Most readers only read the first story, and the number of readers decreases with every passing word and page. Web sites know this phenomenon well.

If this sounds crazy, consider again the disorganized army from Chapter 1. Imagine that army communicating about every enemy soldier along its front lines and barely addressing the primary, biggest, most successful threat breaking through its left flank. That's exactly what is happening in most IT security education environments. The IT security team acts as if they are providing a general news publication with a mandate to share all the POSSIBLE threats that could impact the organization. That's a mistake. The primary, coordinated goal of all IT security education should be to eradicate the top threats, and then begin again with the next top threats. Anything else is inefficient.

The measure of success for each computer security communications and education effort should be:

- How well does it communicate across the enterprise?

- How well does it communicate effectively to each organizational level or group (i.e. the CEO needs different information than a field employee)?
- How well does it communicate the top successful and most likely threats?
- Can all employees, from the CEO on down, name the top threats in order, if asked?
- How often is it updated?
- How effective is it? Does it assist with minimizing top threats efficiently or are readers tested on understanding and knowledge retention? Is it effective toward all groups?

It is important that the organization determines what topics to communicate based on their own experiences. Every employee and team needs to be on the same page, even if the levels of details are different for each of them. After the topics are determined, an internal team should make specific communications for each level of detail needed for the various groups.

For general education purposes, whether the content is generated internally or bought externally is up to the organization. Internal training sources can more easily be related to actual experiences. External training tends to be more professional and of higher quality. The best solution may be to get an external training source that is focused on your specific top threats.

Better Align Mitigations to the Most Critical Threats

Now that you better understand the top successful threats, you need to better align mitigations to those threats. This is why you did all the previous work. You can use a list of the top threats as a "north star" to direct all other work—threat intelligence, threat detection, inclusive communications— toward finding the most efficient mitigations to align against the biggest threats (focusing on root causes) backed by data.

In a nutshell, after the biggest threats are shared, the gathered group should be able to perform a gap analysis on related intelligence, detection, communication, and mitigations. What is needed to better fight the top threats? Often, it's something you already have. It just requires refocusing efforts and more accuracy.

For example, if unpatched software is your biggest problem, it's usually a handful of unpatched programs causing most of the problems. You'd be better off focusing on those specific programs than trying to patch all programs. Use your existing patch management tools and processes but with a renewed sense of purpose and focus. If someone says a supposed "insurmountable" problem is in the way, surmount it. Think outside of the box! Get senior management involved. Use your data. There are few insurmountable problems, only people who run out of good ideas.

Make sure you don't fall victim to the "vulnerability criticality ranking" problem, where every problem is equally ranked as a top priority. Vendors and vulnerability management programs may rank many vulnerabilities as high priorities because they potentially could be. But a data-driven defender answers the question of which vulnerabilities are causing the current biggest problems and are most likely to cause the future biggest problems in their organization. That answer determines what to concentrate on first and drives everything else.

Then do gap analysis to figure out why your top threats are your top threats. It's something. Figure out what that something is and then figure out how to mitigate it. Your recommended mitigations should drive projects, staffing, budgets, and purchasing.

In most companies there is a huge gap between the biggest cybersecurity problems and how much is spent on them. The world is filled with companies that spend millions of dollars on tiny problems and only tens of thousands on the problems that take down their organization. Most corporations are already very well aware of the biggest issue that eventually takes them down long before it happens. It's the disorganized army problem.

Increase Accountability

Periodically, every mitigation should be examined for fitness, how well it is doing at mitigating the found problem. Is the mitigation doing better or worse than the vendor or sponsor said it would do?

To do that, the people proposing the mitigation should also come up with an appropriate metric that can be used to measure its success or lack of it. The metric should be measured before a mitigation or improvement is put in place and then measured and reported again during its review. If the mitigation is falling short, the vendor or sponsor should say why and vice-versa. The idea is to think about outcomes and measurement metrics ahead of time, so that accountability can be empirically measured. This can't be done all the time, but it can be done far more often than is currently tried.

It's important that the right metrics are used and the right questions are asked. Sponsors and employees must have enough resources to install the mitigation correctly and to operate it over its lifetime. Far too many mitigations get installed with much fanfare and then die in a vacuum of operational neglect. Accountability reviews help determine the success of the mitigation. How well the mitigation helps in decreasing the top threats helps with the gap analysis. Depending on the mitigation's success, it may stay, be incrementally improved, removed, or replaced.

Summary

Chapter 4 discussed how to improve nearly any computer security defense plan by getting and utilizing better data, concentrating on the right things, and better aligning mitigations to the biggest successful threats they are supposed to oppose. Chapter 5, "A DDD Example", will discuss a common IT security problem and how applying a data-driven defense can improve the process and significantly reduce risk.

5 A DDD Example

Chapter 5 uses the very common, but complex, IT security task of patch management as an example discussion of how to use a data-driven defense to efficiently decrease security risk.

> *"One experiment is worth a thousand expert opinions."*— Unknown, similar but not identical attributions to Albert Einstein, Wernher Von Braun, and Adm. Grace Murray Hopper

As discussed in Chapter 3, "Broken Defenses", security defenders are expected to be educated and worried about 5,000–15,000 distinct software and firmware vulnerabilities each year. About one-fourth to one-third of vulnerabilities are ranked with the highest risk criticality and over one-third are considered easy to exploit.

Traditional Patch Management

A traditional patch management plan dictates that critical vulnerabilities be patched as soon as is possible, and most organizations set a goal of applying all critical patches within one week to one month of their release by the vendor. Most defenders currently agree that they can wait up to a few days or even a week to see if the applied patches cause critical problems as evidenced by the fastest, earliest appliers of those patches. The vast majority of organizations try to apply critical security patches within one month of their availability.

A minority of organizations require that critical patches be applied on a far longer schedule, sometimes allowing critical patches to be applied as late as many months after their release by the vendor. They justify the longer waiting periods to prevent unexpected and unnecessary operational interruptions. Usually these organizations have been the victim of a previous operation-critical interruption due to an applied problematic security patch and have decided to err on the side of operational interruption versus security.

There are many, usually smaller, organizations with no formal patch management process that either rarely apply patches or only apply them on an ad hoc basis. Some percentage of users are unaware of patching and/or never patch. Hence, each announced vulnerability is a valid attack vector into their systems.

The typical operating system has more than a hundred, sometimes many hundreds, of separate security patches to apply each year. Most organizations support several operating systems and several versions of each of them, plus many dozens to hundreds of applications. They can easily have hundreds of different firmware components that may need patching, and all of these things need to be patched across traditional devices and computers, cloud computer assets, networking equipment, virtual machines, and, if used, containers and microservices. There's a good chance that if a device consumes energy, it needs to be patched. It seems that the only thing that doesn't need patching are humans, and that point is debatable.

In most organizations, anywhere from one person to a few teams are tasked with managing and operating the patch management system. They are responsible for rolling out patches on an agreed-upon service level across all computers and devices within their management sphere. They provide reports back to management detailing the success and failure rates of particular types of devices and software programs. In most cases, if the patch management admins are achieving fairly high rates of overall success, say 95–99% (no one gets 100% success for long), then everyone from senior management on down is pretty happy. That is until a missed patch allows a very damaging successful compromise.

Leaks in the Dike

In my 30+ years of experience, "high rates of successful patching" usually means that the patch management administrators have a fairly high rate of successfully patching OS-critical patches and almost nothing else. Most of the time even the rates of successfully patching OS vulnerabilities are overstated in the patching reports. Management usually believes that OS applications are 95–100% patched, but when I've individually checked each machine or device, rarely have I found a single computer fully patched. It is very common for me to find missing critical OS patches on domain controllers, file servers, and other critical infrastructure servers (e.g. DNS, DHCP, etc.). I also commonly find exploitable management software, missing software drivers, and older, no-longer-patchable software programs.

Workstations often have many high-risk browser programs such as Adobe Acrobat, Oracle Java, Adobe Flash, and other popular add-ons that are not patched. It is very common for a large organization to have five or more versions of popular add-ons widespread across their enterprise, many of which are no longer supported by the vendor and will never be patched. They just remain exploitable.

The patch management team is often not allowed to patch applications and application servers, as that is supposed to be handled by the application managers or owners. The patch management team is usually unaware of the patching rates of those applications and servers, although if checked, those rates are far below the higher rates of the software they are allowed to patch.

In general, if all the patchable devices and software programs are considered, the patch management team is actually only responsible for patching a small subset of everything. Other teams are responsible for patching network equipment and other devices. Those teams patch those devices inconsistently, rarely, or even never. I have never encountered a fully patched network router in an operational network.

Often the managers of these services and servers are acutely aware of the missing patches, but it has been decided that the missing patches would not be applied, for reasons that are not as solid as they would like to believe. Many times, they have very vocal opponents who want all the missing patches applied but are overruled by the majority or senior managers.

Generally speaking, hardware and firmware are rarely patched in any reasonable timeframe, even when critical patches should be applied. Most patch management systems do not check for or report missing firmware patches. Even if they do, firmware is difficult to patch because each firmware type has a different patching routine and requires a reboot of the device. When I was involved in patching one large organization's BIOS firmware for a specific security project, it was determined that the organization had more than 8,000 different firmware versions with over 5,000 separate patching routines that had to be checked and programmed for. It was a logistical nightmare.

Many devices, even if they contain critical vulnerabilities, cannot be patched. This is particularly common in security "appliances". An appliance is usually a computer running a custom-version of a Linux or BSD distribution. While the vendor commonly says that the appliance's OS is "hardened", the reality is that it is rarely patched and usually contains many vulnerabilities, over time growing to number in the dozens or hundreds. Appliance administrators usually aren't even aware that the appliances they are running have vulnerabilities, and they don't or can't check them for missing patches.

Even if appliance administrators were able to discover the missing patches, the appliance vendor does not allow customers to apply them. It likely voids the support contact if the application administrator applies the patch against the wishes of the appliance vendor. When I was a full-time penetration tester, one of my favorite hacking methods was to attack the very security appliances that the customer had bought to protect their environment.

In reality, most environments have a very mixed rate of patching, where the real patching rates are far lower than the "official" reported patching rates. Most patch management team members are aware of this and usually have shared their concerns only to be told that it isn't their problem and they should stop bringing it up.

Multiple teams are responsible for patching different things, and if a patch is missed, they often point fingers at each other. There is often misplaced accountability and responsibility. Even those who are responsible for patching particular devices and software cannot accomplish the patching that they want to. Most organizations actually have very poor patching overall. Penetration testers and hackers know this, which is why unpatched software has for decades been one of the top two reasons that a data breach occurs.

Data-Driven Defense Patch Management

A data-driven computer defense is all about aligning mitigations against the biggest successful threats. Most computers are compromised by social engineering, which has nothing to little to do with vulnerabilities. Unpatched vulnerabilities, however, are the second leading cause of data breaches.

In the vulnerability world, even though there are thousands of new vulnerabilities each year, perhaps a dozen exploits are used against most organizations. If those exploits were 100% patched, those organizations would be better protected than if they patched a far greater number of vulnerabilities semi-well. This is because most malware families and exploit kits check for and often use the same popularly UNPATCHED software, including Adobe Acrobat, Oracle Java, Microsoft Silverlight, and Microsoft Internet Explorer. Even within those software programs they tend to look for and exploit a very limited number of vulnerabilities. For example, even though Internet Explorer may have dozens of new vulnerabilities each year, maybe a handful of them get publicly exploited.

Narrowing Down Worrisome Vulnerabilities

The vulnerabilities you need to worry about are the ones that have exploit code used "in the wild" against real-world targets.

Nothing else really matters as much. Yes, you must worry about zero days, but zero days are a very small part of the risk.

As discussed in Chapter 3, "Broken Defenses", there are about 5,000–16,000 distinct software and firmware vulnerabilities each year (as shown below).

Thousands of new vulnerabilities per year

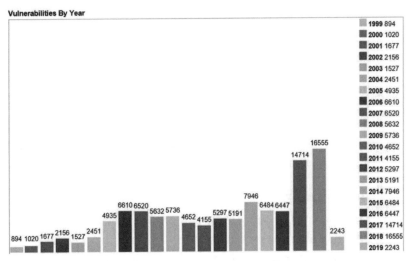

But of those thousands of new vulnerabilities each year, fewer than half (about 30–40%) have public exploit code developed to take advantage of them. Of greater importance, less than 2% (100-320) of them have exploit code that ends up being executed "in the wild" (see the figure below).

Vulnerability statistics from Kenna Security

Comparison of CVEs with exploit code and/or observed exploits in the wild relative to all published CVEs

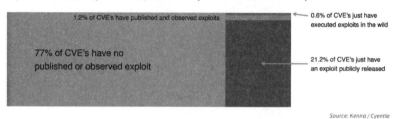

Source: Kenna / Cyentia

But even the 2% figure isn't filtered enough for your organization. Of the public exploits that exist "in the wild", only the unpatched software that exists in your environment is of real concern. In many cases, your organization is not going to even have all the exploitable software in your environment. In other cases, you may have the exploitable software in your environment, but attacks against it are already mitigated.

For example, when unpatched Oracle Java was all the hacking rage, many organizations responded by blocking all Java applets downloaded via Internet browsers or only letting company-preapproved Java applets be executed (getting rid of most of the risk). Just because your organization has vulnerable software in your environment, that doesn't mean it's readily exploitable. In fact, something different is often true. When software is exploitable in your environment, it means there is an environmental weakness that the exploit is taking advantage of.

With the Java example, even during the years when unpatched Java was 90% of most exploits, there were companies that remained unaffected by it. They either didn't have it installed, patched it 100%, or had other mitigations that took away most or all of the risk.

A data-driven defense understands this and focuses mostly on the vulnerabilities that are likely to be exploited "in the wild" and in particular to be successful against your organization.

> Note: Since the first edition of this book was published, I have become aware of security companies that completely understand and focus on this concept of focusing on the right priorities, including Kenna Security (https://www.kennasecurity.com).

Using a data-driven defense, defenders can see that they need primarily worry about vulnerabilities with exploit code "in the wild", and even then only for the software in their environment without any other offsetting mitigations.

Most Commonly Attacked Software Components

Over the last two decades, a clear pattern of what attackers focus on when exploiting unpatched software has emerged, and the pattern differs depending on whether they are attacking workstations or servers.

Most attacked unpatched software is usually Internet-facing/accessing.

For clients, the unpatched software is usually:

- Internet browser add-ons

- Network-advertising services/daemons

- OS

- Productivity applications (Microsoft Office, etc.)

For servers, the unpatched software is usually:

- Web server software

- OS

- Database software

- Server management software

In most environments, unless you have a history or expectation to counteract this claim, these are the types of software you should focus on patching first and best.

A Tough Question

Now that you are a data-driven defense expert, let me propose a scenario to you along with a tough question. Suppose you are told about some MAJOR vulnerability that, if exploited, can completely take over nearly every computer and device in your environment, and the only defense is patching it right away. Should you immediately patch that severe vulnerability at the cost of giving up all other patches or just continue business as usual and focus on patching the things that are already most likely to be exploited? This is the type of tough question that a data-driven defense begs you to evaluate.

This is not a hypothetical scenario. These situations come along every decade or so, and the vulnerability involved is so dire that the consequences involved are almost unimaginable. Two such vulnerabilities were discovered in 2017. The Meltdown and Spectre (https://meltdownattack.com/) vulnerabilities were due to chip- or firmware-level flaws that impacted most CPU chips manufactured since 1995, and they could be exploited on nearly any OS against almost any device that used those chips (including smart phones). The exploit could not be stopped by any anti-malware program, and its exploitation would not be noted on any security log. Exploit code and videos were created to demonstrate both exploits. There probably hasn't been a worse nightmare-scenario vulnerability ever announced.

Official Meltdown and Spectre icons

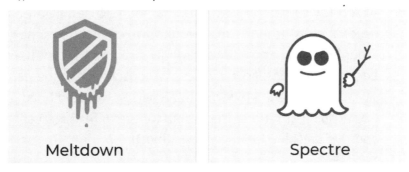

So, the question is this: If you were around when Meltdown and Spectre were announced, should you drop what you were doing with your regular patch management plans and patch Meltdown and Spectre, even if it meant not patching 100% of the things you've been told are more likely to be exploited? I asked this exact question at several security conferences at the time.

What is a security defender to do?

As bad as those vulnerabilities sound, unless the exploit code ends up being used "in the wild", you probably don't have to worry about it so much. Based on decades of data, you are most likely to be exploited in the same ways that you have recently been exploited and are most likely to be exploited in the future. Returning to the army allegory from Chapter 1, I believe that Meltdown and Spectre were like the supposed aerial attacks the good army was told to worry about instead of putting more resources and troops on the left flank. There are a lot of things that you are going to be told are critical emergencies that you absolutely must worry about and fix right now. The data-driven defender's job is to figure out which things are the real emergencies to worry about. And for that, use your history, experience, and data.

At security conferences where I told people that they probably needn't worry as much about Meltdown or Spectre as they thought, many in the crowd strongly disagreed. I was often booed. I was once led early out of a consulting engagement for saying the same thing because the person who had hired me was pushing as hard as they could for senior management to approve patching Meltdown and Spectre.

The result? Two years later, Meltdown and Spectre still had not been publicly exploited. Many early adopters ended up causing their computers to crash, lock, or at best, run significantly slower. It turns out that the fixes to patch Meltdown and Spectre were far more complicated than the chip manufacturers and OS vendors had initially thought. Customers who applied the critical patches that the vendors so strongly recommended ended up with lots of operational issues against a backdrop of zero public exploits.

What if a DDD Conclusion Is Wrong?

Imagine that Meltdown and Spectre actually had led to public exploits and that the data-driven followers who had waited to patch it consequently ended up getting exploited? Wouldn't that prove that the data-driven approach is flawed and failed in this instance? Can't an attacker at any time choose to attack a victim in any possible way, past history, facts, and data be damned?

Yes.

It is possible that an attacker could buck conventional wisdom and do something entirely new or unexpected. It is possible that Meltdown and Spectre might have turned into a world-wide catastrophe of exploits.

That still doesn't make a data-driven computer defense wrong. A data-driven defense is about making your best estimations, based on actual experience and data, to predict what the most likely future attacks will be. It's all about concentrating on the best odds. Concentrating on the biggest threats that are most likely to happen is the right approach no matter what the outcome is. Yes, there might be particular "by-the-gut" defenders who get lucky over a data-driven approach, much like the lucky few stock market pickers who occasionally pick a market upturn or downturn correctly. But you never see them do it twice. Most of the time it was sheer luck on timing.

Returning to our army allegory, should a real army ever focus on the least likely attack scenarios to the detriment of the current and most likely to occur attacks? No, of course not. We already know how that is working out with today's traditional computer defenses, which is not so well.

Conclusion

Using a data-driven computer defense, defenders can go from worrying about 5,000–16,000 vulnerabilities to focusing on just a dozen or so. A data-driven computer defense wants all IT security implementations to be risk-driven the same way, be they patch management, security awareness training, secure development lifecycle training, or authentication solutions. A data-driven defense knows that your organization will better and faster decrease security risk by focusing on the highest risk things first and best.

Chapter 5 used patch management as an example to further study and refine data-driven defenses. Chapter 9, "More Implementation Examples", will explore many more examples that can be used to help implement your own data-driven defenses. Chapter 6, "Asking the Right Questions", will help you ask the right questions to get the right data-driven defense outcomes.

6 Asking the Right Questions

Chapter 6 discusses the importance of asking the right security questions for a data-driven defense.

> *"If I had an hour to solve a problem and my life depended on the solution, I would spend the first 55 minutes determining the proper question to ask, for once I know the proper question I could solve the problem in less than 5 minutes."*—Albert Einstein

The Importance of Asking the Right Questions

The Einstein quote above basically says it all. If you ask the right questions, you can usually get the right solutions faster. The most important discoverers in history contained an innate thirst to answer basic questions that had long been on their mind. Many described their ability to ask questions with child-like curiosity as the secret to their success. They wondered why the sky was blue or why apples always fell to the ground, and they decided not to take "I dunno" or someone's obvious best guess as an answer.

A Microsoft SDL Example

I'll use my previous employer, Microsoft, as an example of why asking the right questions is so important. Early on, Microsoft was not known as an OS vendor absolutely focused on computer security to the exclusion of all else. Some older readers might be chuckling at my politically correct understatement. But 20–30 years ago, few vendors focused on computer security. Computer attacks were not even a huge problem. Today's antivirus scanners had not even been invented, and the most damaging computer worms took down only thousands of computers. The Internet wasn't even the Internet then.

Microsoft thought it was doing a great job security-wise and certainly no better or worse than any other vendor. But their incredibly large market share, very popular products, and Internet-connectedness began to attract a lot of hackers and malware. In a matter of a few years, their customers routinely suffered from attacks that exploited millions of computers in a single day. These were the days of the Code Red, Iloveyou, and Melissa computer worms and macro viruses, which caused widespread, global interruptions.

Microsoft's reputation started to suffer. The resulting question was "Why are our customers starting to not trust Microsoft software?" The partial answer/metric they could directly control was "the number of critical security bugs per thousand lines of code." Microsoft figured that significantly decreasing the number of bugs in their code would help change their security reputation.

Microsoft began by declaring computer security to be more important than it used to be, particularly regarding coding bugs. This was publicly kicked off by CEO Bill Gates's infamous "Trustworthy Computing" memo (https://www.wired.com/2002/01/bill-gates-trustworthy-computing/) in 2002. It changed the culture of Microsoft to this day.

Microsoft's central push to decrease critical security bugs (created by Michael Howard and David LeBlanc) is known as the

Security Development Lifecycle (SDL), and it is a huge success by any measure. Microsoft's code quickly started to contain far fewer critical bugs, not only per thousands of lines per code, but also overall regardless of the number of lines of code. In any category, Microsoft software has far fewer bugs than its closest competitors. It is extremely common for Microsoft software to have one-third or less of the number of bugs than its competitors have in the same timeframe, across the spectrum. As far as I know, there hasn't been an exception to that statement since 2003. Some major pieces of Microsoft software, like SQL Server or DNS, have gone years without a single security bug, while Microsoft's closest competitors suffered dozens or hundreds in the same time period. Even Microsoft's Internet browsers have fewer bugs than their competitors. These statements usually shock people, but it's the truth, and it is a direct result of the SDL initiative.

Microsoft code has become so secure that the vast majority of successful exploitations to Microsoft Windows computers are not because of Microsoft software bugs. Today, most Microsoft Windows computers are compromised because of unpatched non-Microsoft software and social engineering. Success, success, success. Then a funny thing was noticed.

After all of Microsoft's success at decreasing a key metric and significantly increasing the security of their software across the board, the percentage of their customers being regularly compromised hadn't gone down along with the number of bugs. Instead of Microsoft's software being at fault, it was someone else's software or another method like social engineering, where it's more the case that human behavior is at fault. The fact that it wasn't due to Microsoft software, in particular, didn't make their customers feel any less frustrated.

Microsoft realized that a better new question now wasn't whether their software contained more or fewer security bugs, but whether their customers were compromised to a greater or lesser extent over time, and why.

With that new question, they realized that they had to reach out even more to help all developers write more secure software, and not just developers writing code for the Microsoft Windows platform. Today, Microsoft offers cloud and other services that work across many computing platforms and devices. They doubled down on their SDL strategy and actively seek to help all developers, even their strongest competitors. For example, Microsoft even sent SDL teams to Apple. A happier and safer customer benefits everyone. Microsoft's security mantra became "a rising tide lifts all boats!"

The right questions and answers, when known and supported by data, should drive the rest of the computer security defense plan. Beyond each central question, data needs to provide the answers to the many related, more nuanced questions, each of which seeks to make computer security defense more effective. To ask the right questions, you might have to retrain yourself, your co-workers, and your staff, using a better data-driven security mindset.

The Right Questions to Ask

It's crucial to ask the right questions. The key first question to answer for a data-driven computer defense is "What are the top current and future most likely SUCCESSFUL threats, by damage, to my organization?" As I repeat in nearly every chapter, there is a huge gulf between your biggest POTENTIAL threats and your biggest SUCCESSFUL threats. You want to focus on capturing the latter in your computer security risk plan.

Start by measuring the damage that has occurred from current and recent successful attacks to your company. Then add the most likely to occur future events. You should have these answers from the fundamental gap analysis, discussed in Chapter 4, gained by improved threat intelligence and threat detection.

Many defenders, after years of experiencing traditional security plans, have been unknowingly trained to ask the wrong, although easier to answer, questions. For example, suppose your organization determines that malware is a top threat. What are the right questions to ask? Traditionally, a defender might be tempted to choose the overall number of malware occurrences that have been detected and removed across the enterprise. They might see a sign of increased malware detection and removal as a sign of improvement (i.e. decrease in risk).

But pure numbers alone without more context don't tell the most important parts of the story. Was there an increase in the amount of malware brought into the company as compared to previous periods? That alone might account for an increase in detections, even if the antivirus product's detection rate stays the same (or even decreases).

A Malware Example

If malware is a top threat, one of the best metrics to use is malware accuracy. How accurately is your antivirus product performing now versus previous periods? How long is malware going undetected before being detected (i.e. mean-time-to-detect)? This is actually much easier to figure out than you might think. I'll give you the answer in Chapter 9, "More Implementation Examples".

Continuing, what is the top root cause for malware getting by initial defenses? This is a key question to ask and answer. Suppose you find out that it is unpatched software. Fix that single issue, and your malware numbers should fall as well.

What user or malware actions occurred on the computers and devices while malware was present before the malware was detected and removed? What types of computers are malware most often found on, low-risk or high-risk computers? Did the users perform admin tasks while the malware was present and undetected? Did they pick up confidential email? Did they access high business impact systems and data? Is malware appearing on computers that shouldn't be connecting to the Internet? Is malware detection usually high on particular computers, devices, configurations, or users, and if so, why?

In general, if one of my primary worries is malware, I want to see my antivirus software getting more accurate with faster mean-time-to-detect metrics, especially on my highest risk computers. If mean-time-to-detect is increasing, why? This could indicate that it's time to evaluate a new antivirus vendor.

This is not to say that pure numbers don't mean anything in every case. For example, if social engineering is a top problem, institute mitigations to decrease it and measure social engineering success over time. Even then, I'd want to use metrics to see what forms of social engineering are being the most successful and why. When you understand the biggest problems and why they happen, you can implement the most appropriate mitigations.

You want to figure out your top SUCCESSFUL threats and then ask the right questions and track the right metrics to defeat them. However, be prepared to change both the questions and the answers as the situation requires.

For example, should you care more about the number of malware programs detected and cleaned in your environment or how long it took your anti-malware solutions to detect and remove malware after it was first present? Are all computer malware infection detections treated the same, or should some infections result in forensic investigations because of where they are found (i.e. a data-exfiltrating Trojan is found on the CEO's computer or a credential theft tool on a DC)? Do you care more about the top *potential* threats against your company or the top threats that are *currently* being successful? Do you want to capture more events in your log management system or fine-tune your log management system to be better at alerting you about more likely hacking events? Do you care more about a list of all the ways someone could break into your environment or just the most likely successful ones? A data-driven defense mind wants answers to the latter questions, supported by data.

Should pure numbers of occurrence really mean as much as we often think they do? For example, nearly every company in the world is running an antivirus product that is capable of giving you up-to-the-second reports on the names of malware found and how many were detected and removed in a given time period.

If an antivirus system tells you it found and removed 1 million malware programs this month versus 1.1 million last month, is that data point super valuable? I'll argue that without the appropriate context it is not. What was the antivirus's detection accuracy? How many malware programs should it have detected? Were more malware programs found on more critical computers this month versus the prior month? How long did the existing malware programs exist before the antivirus software detected them? Is the "mean-time-to-detect" rising or falling over time? What types of programs were they? Simple adware, run-of-the-mill Trojans, bitcoin generators, or data-exfiltrating Trojans? Were more data-exfiltrating Trojans found on sensitive data computers this month versus last month? What were the root causes of how the malware got to people's computers in the first place, and in what percentages? What are the lessons we can learn from the instances of critical failures? Is there anything we can learn from and fix to improve prevention or detection accuracy?

Asking the Right Questions

A data-driven defender needs to question everything and ask the right questions. The world's most famous scientists often claim a big part of their success was due to them continuing to wonder like a child and asking questions that everyone else ceased to ask a long time ago. The central common question they are pondering is "Why does this happen?" They then begin to figure out which things do or don't impact the expected outcome of whatever it is they are investigating.

Once you begin to think about computer security defense using data-ranked priorities, you'll never want to drive a project using the older, more traditional, less valuable questions that are based on pure numbers or gut instincts alone. You'll hate unranked lists of threats or projects. You'll cringe whenever someone tells you to change the order of your top priorities without providing you with compelling data to clearly demonstrate why it is needed. You'll innately see where the data gaps are or where better data is needed to provide better confidence to do something. You don't want to do something just to be busy. You want to do the right things at the right time! In a data-driven defense plan, data is king! Data analysts are the rock stars! Gut feelings are for suckers.

A Data-Driven Consulting Example

Here's a real-life example that I experienced that demonstrates the value you can add by always thinking "data-driven defense". I was consulting at a large, Fortune 50 company and meeting with a very skeptical CSO. His company had sustained multiple, very damaging hacker intrusions over the last decade. No matter what they tried—and they had spent hundreds of millions of dollars—it did not stop hackers from gaining unauthorized access to their systems. The CSO was understandably frustrated.

I started by asking simple questions that every (data-driven defense-minded) CSO should know off the top of their head, including:

- What cyberthreat causes the most damage against your company?
- What systems can detect that threat? How accurately? How many false-positives do they provide? Do people respond to every reported detection instance or is the data ignored most of the time?
- Is the mean-time-to-detect that threat going up or down over time?
- Does everyone on your team understand the top threats and their causes?
- How much of your end-user education material is devoted to discussing and preventing the top threats?

- Which mitigations are most effective against the top threats?

I kept asking questions into a lengthening silence. I could tell he was growing frustrated because he didn't have the answers. I told him that it was critical for him to figure out what the best questions to ask and answer were in order to best measure the security of his company. I told him that I had a good idea about what his company's biggest cyber problems were, but that he needed to get better data to help prioritize his ongoing efforts. I gave him examples of how I had helped companies empirically measure their true risk and to more quickly minimize their biggest weaknesses.

But I think he misinterpreted my data-driven thought-process as mocking him and his current team's attempts to ferret out maliciousness. He might also have thought that for the money he was paying for my services that I would be able to tell him specifically what he should be concentrating on, using data and experience from previous customers. He wanted me to be able to say something like "You should patch Adobe better and hold one-hour social engineering classes" or something like that. But I told him that without seeing his company's own data and experiences, I could not tell him what to fix first or how.

With that reply, he literally threw a report at me in frustration. The report was an unranked list of the 20 ways his red team (i.e. professional team of employees hired to hack a company's defenses to find vulnerabilities before malicious hackers do) had successfully hacked into his company's servers. The report basically said "You need to go fix these 20 critical things right now!"

Exasperated, he asked "So, which one of these 20 things do I need to fix first?" I said "Exactly! Without good data no one knows! Does this report even have the value you think it has? Does it have any relevance to how real-world hackers are currently breaking into your environment or are most likely to do so in the near future? Which vulnerabilities are tied to the most damage? What are the growing threat trends? If you had these answers, it would tell you which vulnerabilities you need to be concentrating on."

No one can simultaneously concentrate on 20 top priorities. I don't care who you are or how much money and how many employees you have. It just can't be done. You'll be lucky to be able to concentrate on and fix one or a few things in a given year. Using an unranked list of cyber issues that are not backed by real-world data does not come close to being efficient. Any unordered list of things to fix without data to support what you should be concentrating on first should be seen as inefficient and likely inaccurate. What you concentrate on first should be supported by actual data of successful current and most likely future attacks.

Red team activities do not necessarily reflect real-world attacks. Red teams usually have innate knowledge and experience that isn't shared with real-world attackers. Consciously or unconsciously, many red teams concentrate on threats that they think the company should be most worried about, but the prioritization of those risks unfortunately is not usually driven and supported by real-world, specific, local data.

Defenders need to start with better information about how their organization is attacked by real, current day attackers, ranked by damage or potential chance of damage. Real, successful current attacks, followed by the most likely future events, should take precedence over everything else. Identifying this information requires asking the right questions, performing data collection, and doing analysis. Any unordered, unranked list that lacks supporting data should be given less precedence for action or at least should be viewed skeptically.

Data is king! Data should drive most decisions. Data analysts should become the rock stars in your organization. A new culture of data-driven defense should start to be built and pervade the organization. A new computer security mindset should start to permeate the IT organization and lead the culture. Everything else should be driven by the data, just as it is in the insurance and other industries. Data analysts should be seen as the valuable assets that they are. In important areas and decisions, try to get data where you did not have it before. Get better data where you had weak data. Think in a data-driven way. Start to ask the right questions.

Data-Driven Mantras and Questions
Here are some of my "data is king" mantras and questions that I share with all my customers and students:

- Data is the conduit of success.

- Learn to ask the right questions.

- Define metrics. If you can't measure it, you can't rank or manage it.

- Gut feelings should be backed up by data.

- A key metric is determining root causes.

- What defenses would help the most?

- What gaps do you have in detection, measuring, and reporting?

- How is your organization successfully broken into the most today? What causes the most damage?

- What are the most likely successful hacking events against your organization, after looking at the current and future most likely successful events?

- What are the trends? What's increasing? What's decreasing? What's improving? What's not? Why?

- How well does everyone in your organization understand the top successful threats?

- Are the big deployed mitigations successful against the top most damaging threats? How well do they match up?

- Are vendors and sponsors held accountable for delivering on what they have promised?

One of my favorite exercises to generate more of the right questions is to ask each team in the organization "What question or questions if answered would help you do a better job defending the organization?" Usually they are stunned into silence. They haven't been asked that type of question before. Tell them to take ten minutes and try to come up with three questions they would like to know the answer to. Give them some examples from this book. Most of the time you'll get some good questions they want answered. They may ask how you can possibly get the answers to those questions, but the point is to brainstorm to find out what questions and answers are most critical to those teams. Then evaluate each proposed question to see if it really is valuable and worth pursuing.

Sometimes teams are so stuck in the old, non-data-driven world that they can't even think of the best questions to ask. But you can help facilitate their journey. Then after figuring out which are the best questions, start to work on what it would take to answer them.

Chapter 6 was about asking the right questions to get a better data-driven defense. Chapter 7, "Getting Better Data", is about getting better data to answer those good questions.

7 Getting Better Data

Chapter 7 explores what constitutes reliable computer security defense data, gives examples, and summarizes log management basics.

> "Fiction is obliged to stick to possibilities. Truth isn't."
> —Mark Twain

Creating a computer security defense plan based on data means you have to ask the right questions, get the right data and metrics to answer them, and feel confident that your choices are reliable indicators of your organization's real security posture and risk. It's not easy. It's the reason why most traditional computer security defense plans rely more on gut feelings, guesses, and unexpected external influences than data. But it can be done.

A data-driven defender expects changes to occur over time. Threats change. Questions change. Answers change. Make sure you are using good data to support the changes.

What Makes Good Data for Data Points?

The computer security world doesn't hurt for data. The average computer generates thousands to hundreds of thousands of log events each day. Firewalls drop thousands of unauthorized network packets every day. Antivirus scanners process hundreds of thousands of files each day. Nearly all computers and devices are generating an astounding number of log messages. The average enterprise is generating billions of new security event messages each day. The question is "How much of that information is useful and valuable?"

The answer is that most of this data is useless "noise" that could never be used to make a significant computer security decision or alert. Unfortunately, many of the useless messages are generated by default, can't easily be turned off, and are required by a small minority of scenarios as part of a guideline, certification requirement, or law. We may hate all the noise, but it doesn't mean we can easily get rid of it. So, what makes a good security event data point?

Data Should Be Reliable

To start with, the data should be reliable. This means that a log message is generated every time the same event occurs, contains useful information, is marked with an accurate time stamp, and is resistant to unauthorized, malicious modification or interruption. Most security logs meet this requirement.

Data Should Be Useful

If the data could not lead to detecting a malicious security event or generating an alert, it should be discontinued if possible. Most computer logs are thin on useful events. Unfortunately, most users cannot control what event messages are or aren't generated by a computer or device. However, users and administrators can determine what event messages to monitor and retrieve from a particular computer or device. I'm a big fan of letting computers log as much information as they want but only retrieving, collating, and alerting on a much smaller data set.

When I see companies brag about how many event messages per second they collect or how big their event log management hard drive arrays are, that usually means they aren't being very selective. It often indicates that their network traffic and event management systems are processing too much useless information. These are generally the same companies that have to wait minutes for an answer when they execute a query against their event log management system. I don't want to criticize this occurrence too badly because, sadly, this situation is by far the norm in most organizations.

Data Should Be Actionable and Help Remediate Top Threats

The data should be as specific and actionable as possible for the scenario and should help to remediate the top successful or most likely threats. For example, instead of reporting on overall patch compliance status, report on the top unpatched applications that are linked to the top successful threats. Telling someone that the organization is 95% in compliance with patching doesn't provide super useful information, even if that compliance used to be only 90% and is improving. That could represent better patching on an application that is rarely exploited even while a more likely to be exploited application is actually falling in compliance. If unpatched software is a top threat to your organization, name the top applications involved, and focus on getting better patch compliance on those.

If malware is a problem, a good metric and goal is to decrease the mean-time-to-detect malware over time. Another good goal is to decrease occurrences on servers or other high-risk machines. If social engineering is a top problem, you could conduct simulated social engineering tests centered on the number one social engineering problem. Does your selected metric fall or rise over time as expected?

Traits of a Good Computer Security Event

A perfect data event to create security alerts should contain the following attributes:

- It must be able to be used to detect malicious events.
- Either a single occurrence or an unexpected change from the baseline number of events in a given time period indicates a high chance of unauthorized activity.
- It has a low number of false-positives and false-negatives.
- It is readily understood by receivers/viewers.
- An occurrence should be important enough to result in an investigative/forensics action.

All of these attributes are related to one another—it's hard to have one of them without the others. Sadly, for too many security event messages, none of these attributes are true. The average computer security log is full of event messages that miss most or all of these attributes. If an event message lacks these attributes, then it should not be picked up and dropped off at a centralized event log management system (unless required by control, regulation, or law).

Personally, I prefer to leave useless event messages on the local device to avoid taxing the network or cluttering up storage drives. Most of the time you can't turn them off locally or they are needed for possible forensic investigations. That's okay. Leave them stored locally as you always have done. But if there's no requirement to retrieve them into a centralized event log management system, don't.

Exercise: Define 10 Events

Most event log systems I review are full of "noise" and false-positives. Most of the time defenders are overwhelmed with trying to find the truly malicious events. When I see that, I challenge the defenders to review each event message against the five traits I listed in the preceding section. And if an event message can't be justified, then stop collecting it.

Initially, as a good data-driven defense exercise, I challenge teams to identify 10 computer security events that, if detected, would absolutely mean a malicious act is taking place. Here are some examples:

- Someone tries to logon as Administrator when no such account exists (i.e. the built-in Administrator account has been renamed to something else).
- Someone tries to logon as anyone to a honeypot (e.g. "fake" computer or device deployed as an early warning sensor).
- Thousands of failed logons occur across multiple high-value computers far above the normal base number of failed logons (which could be indicating a password spray attack).
- If server A should never normally connect to Server B, alert when they connect to each other.
- If normal network traffic between point A and point B is 1GB per day and all of a sudden it jumps to 100GB, research it.
- If your company never sends files to China and suddenly hundreds of gigabits of data are headed to China, you might want to check that out.
- If you run RDP on a non-default port (say port 63389 instead of 3389), alert when someone connects on 3389.
- If employees in factory location A never do work at night, alert when a user logs on at night.
- If you have no members in your Domain Admins group and someone suddenly appears as an admin there, have someone check that out immediately.

What is guaranteed to be anomalous varies by organization, but the goal is to come up with a nice selection of "guaranteed-to-be" malicious hacker or malware events.

Ten isn't a magic number. Sometimes I say five or twenty, depending on the maturity of the team and their interest in the exercise. I just put out a number to give the team an achievable goal and get the process started. Once they achieve this goal and see the benefits, it's easier to rework the entire system.

> Note: A great, brand new Windows event log management book is Andrei Miroshnikov's *Windows Security Monitoring: Scenarios and Patterns* book (https://www.amazon.com/Windows-Security-Monitoring-Scenarios-Patterns/dp/1119390648). I worked with Andrei at Microsoft and tech edited the book for Wiley.

Highest Echelon of Computer Security Data

The goal of data-driven defense is not only to have good data tied to the top threats and their mitigations, but to more easily communicate the information learned from that data to all levels of stakeholders. Different groups and levels need different things.

Personally, the best overall technical data communication mechanism I've seen was something I first encountered many years ago in a popular application control program, Bit9's Parity (now renamed and part of Carbon Black [https://www.carbonblack.com/]). Parity had this great feature where every single computer it protected was compared to the company's example baseline. The baseline was basically a list of all approved programs before the computer was handed out to end-users. A brand new, unmodified PC, with only approved programs installed, would have a risk score of 0.

Parity kept track of all the programs that appeared over time beyond the baseline on each managed PC. It even assigned a "risk rating" to each recognized program. Malware programs were ranked very high, popularly attacked programs were ranked next highest, and everything else more moderately. Each PC also got a "drift" risk rating that essentially told any interested party how much the PC had drifted from the original baseline and what additional risk the PC had accumulated. A user or admin could quickly review the PC and every new file not on the baseline for an individual risk rating.

Each PC was gathered into a recognizable group, usually representing a location, device type, OS version, department, business unit, and so on. Each group had an accumulated risk score depending on all the individual PCs assigned to it (and their individual scores). Each group could be gathered into other larger groups until they all eventually rolled up into a single risk value that was assigned to the entire managed entity. Any allowed stakeholder could quickly see the company's accumulated risk rating over time and drill down into any necessary detail to see what was making the entire entity's score go up or down. If the risk rating went down over time, then all stakeholders could breathe a little easier. I've never seen a better report or system. It was revolutionary for its time, although I've seen similar reporting mechanisms now in other computer security software.

For example, the software at KnowBe4, Inc., where I currently work, has a feature called the Virtual Risk Officer™ that examines several user attributes of risk (including whether the user's passwords are on the Internet, how many security awareness training classes they have taken, how many simulated phishing tests they have failed or passed, etc.) to give each user an overall personal risk score (see the figure below).

Example KnowBe4 individual risk score

Personal Risk Score

That score can move up or down depending on how the user is doing in the various risk categories over time. Each individual risk score can be wrapped up into larger groups, such as a department, a location, or even the entire organization. You can then generate an overall risk score for the organization (see the example figure below). It's unique in the security training awareness world, and I'm very proud of my company for making this feature.

Example KnowBe4 organization risk score

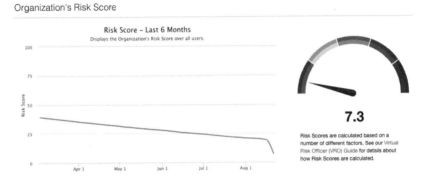

In my perfectly envisioned dream world, stakeholders could get a risk rating for all their top threats/risks and root causes. They would get individual ratings on all the different defenses a computer or device has (e.g. end-user training, anti-malware, encryption, privacy, application control, firewall, authentication, patch status, network security, etc.). Those individual numbers for each different system would roll up into a single risk rating for the system and then roll up again until it provided a single value for the whole company. Then all stakeholders could look at a single screen, such as a dashboard app, and see the overall value or drill down as needed.

The highest echelon report for a data-driven defense would be a single report or dashboard that reports on the top current and most likely successful threats and the metrics and mitigations surrounding each. Using the right metrics, the report would show the occurrence numbers or damage from each threat and then indicate whether they are going up or down over time.

When I'm designing a data-driven defense plan and trying to decide how to capture the right data, my goal is to mimic as closely as possible the highest echelon of data security analytics that I'm discussing here. It's very difficult to accomplish, but if you shoot for this as a "stretch goal", you're more likely to achieve something close or at least much better than what you have today.

Log Management 101

This section of the chapter provides a brief introduction to general log management theory. Event log management allows you to quantitatively and proactively measure the overall health of your environment, from a security perspective, for auditing and compliance, for systems management, and for application tuning and troubleshooting. This section focuses on security event log management only.

> Note: This section doesn't include any special recommendations or hints specific to a data-driven defense and is only included here to ground the reader in log management concepts. If you are already very familiar with log management basics, you can skip ahead to the next chapter.

Security event monitor logging can alert incident response teams so they can prevent malicious hacking in the first place or at least send in the cavalry as quickly as possible after an exploitative event has occurred to minimize damage and start forensic investigations.

NIST SP 800-92

Logging security events for intrusion detection and forensics, which is often the main reason administrators get into log management, requires specialized advice. Readers unfamiliar with the basics should start by reading NIST's Special Publication 800-92, "Guide to Computer Security Log Management" (https://csrc.nist.gov/publications/detail/sp/800-92/final). Released in September 2006, it's unusually easy to read for a NIST (National Institute of Standards and Technology) publication and extremely useful for deploying event log management systems in the real world. It's considered the gospel in this small corner of the computer security world.

NIST Log File Management Essentials

The NIST guide steps through all of the essentials of log file management, analysis, and preparation, including:

1. Identifying the threats and risks to the monitored environment
2. Determining audit policies for logging
3. Auditing and handling logs
4. Collating, indexing, and normalizing logs for analysis
5. Defining and generating alerts and actions for critical events
6. Defining reports and metrics for management review

From putting log management infrastructure and processes into place to reviewing and archiving logs, SP 800-92 leaves no stone unturned.

Log Management Operational Lifecycle

Enterprise log management has nine distinct operational phases:

1. Configuration
2. Collection
3. Normalization
4. Indexing
5. Storage
6. Correlation
7. Baselining
8. Alerting
9. Reporting

You may see the various phases summarized in different ways, but the lifecycle is always the same. The following sections examine the lifecycle phases in slightly more detail.

Configuration

Along with the event log management system itself, every participating host or device will need to be configured. You'll need to investigate the possible event messages that a particular computer or device generates and learn how to configure the event log service to generate actionable events. How often are event messages generated and transmitted, either in real time or via batch files? What fields of information are included, and what do they mean? What is the log file format, and in what ways can the file be assembled and sent? Event logging attributes may or may not be configurable, although here are some common traits and sample decisions that usually are:

- How big do you configure local log files or how long do you keep them?
- When should they overwrite the previous logs, and should overwriting be performed first in, first out, by date, or using some other rotation method?

- Do you keep extracted log events, and if so, what events, how long, and by what method? Some entities must keep all generated security events (which is quite a chore and requires lots of storage space). You might also be tasked with keeping events for legal or forensic reasons, which might require that all written events be saved on unmodifiable media when first written.

Determining the answer to such questions, and even finding the right questions to answer, can take a tremendous amount of effort.

Collection

Manual enterprise event monitoring is very difficult to accomplish beyond a handful of computers and devices. In order to be efficient and productive, you are going to want to round up all the logs (or as many as possible) into a single collection point. The initial reaction is usually to collect all event messages to the centralized location, and this is perhaps the safest option from a security perspective. But can your centralized collection source handle the volume, network-wise, transaction-wise, and storage-wise? Without appropriate testing, networks and event log collection systems have buckled under a few hundred to thousand computer logs being collected.

Some data-driven defense-enabled event log administrators may decide to collect only the most critical, actionable event messages into the centralized event log system, leaving most other event messages behind on the local system. As long as the local event logs are appropriately sized, the administrator should be able to correlate the bigger event logs with the centralized system if needed. This is a strategy that I think best fits most proactive event logging systems.

Alternately, administrators can create a set of branch office collection points that gather all the events from the systems in the nearby vicinity and then forward them to a central collection point or a series of central collection points.

Some administrators and event log systems leave all event logs on the local system and use an event log agent to crawl the local logs when important events need to be queried. This arrangement results in the least amount of network impact but significantly slows down queries and complicates event correlation. The ideal solution should optimize the collection and use of log events for the desired objectives and weigh that against the impact on monitored systems and the network.

Be sure to think of reliability and security. If the central log collection facility goes down, what happens on the local clients? Are event messages dropped and lost forever, or are they cached and transmitted when the central system comes back online? If the central system is down, how long can the local system hold event messages before data is lost? Are logs transmitted securely so that unauthorized eavesdropping doesn't occur? Are logs checked for completeness, the importance of which cannot be understated if your log files end up in a court of law? Are the time clocks between all the monitored systems and the centralized logging system synchronized?

Also, don't forget to make sure the system with event log collection turned on has the accurate time. Event logs with inaccurate dates or times are harder to analyze and more difficult to trust. More and more log systems are tracked and linked by Coordinated Universal Time (UTC) even if the logs are displayed in the local time zone and format. UTC makes log synchronization across time zones easier to coordinate. This is important because if you make one mistake and your data is used in legal proceedings, you'll see the opposing attorney call for dismissal of your data.

Normalization

Normalization of the collected data is perhaps the second most time-consuming phase of event monitoring during the initial configuration. Unless you have only one type of monitored system version (ex. Microsoft Windows 10 OS, etc.), the log files you collect from the disparate systems and versions will not always arrive in the same format or with the same data fields and values. In fact, many environments end up looking like technological equivalents of the Tower of Babel.

Normalization is the process of combining various log file formats and messages into a common schema and optimizing each collected data field into a single database instance or view. A good event log management program handles much of the data normalization for you, using the vendor's years of experience to automate the decisions that most users would commonly select.

Indexing

Before or after normalization, most event log management programs select key fields upon which to index the information for later, faster retrieval. Some log management programs allow any field to be an index, while others lock users into predefined selections. All event log management programs sort by a date/timestamp, placing more recent events above earlier events by default. You need to decide on which event log fields to pull and, from those, which to index on.

Storage

Event logs can easily take up hundreds of gigabytes of data. In fact, many admins saw their first multi-terabyte hard drive when collecting log files. Your event log system not only needs to anticipate the maximum storage size but must also keep track of how long to store event messages. Some administrators need to keep event messages forever. Others are required by corporate policy to delete them after a particular period of time to prevent inadvertent legal discoveries. Some enterprises have a legal requirement, where the data's first stored state must be made permanent, demonstrably so (e.g., write-once, read-many media), and follow a defined chain of custody.

Baselining

Although baselines are not an official phase of many log management operational summaries, it's difficult to discern the noise from the actionable events without understanding your environment's baselines. Every environment is different, with its own natural circadian-like rhythms of peaks and valleys. Baselining is the process of taking log activity measurements over known normal periods of time. Each hour and day will end up with their own baseline, as will monthly cycles.

For example, most networks have increasing levels of logon and network activity from early morning until just before lunch. Because of lunch, activity levels start lowering from 11 a.m. until about 1 p.m., followed by a few hours' rise, only to fall again as the workday ends. On the other hand, 24-hour production shops may see sustained levels at all times—hence, the need for baselining. If you don't know what is normal, how can you define actionable events and alerts?

Correlation

Sophisticated event management systems can automatically identify seemingly disparate event messages and consider them as a single common event. For instance, many companies have enabled lockout policies to disable accounts (and generate lockout alerts for them) that have had their passwords guessed too many times in a given period. Three bad guesses within five minutes is a common lockout threshold.

Hackers will sometimes guess across multiple computers at once against the same account because the account lockout threshold applies on only a given machine. By spreading a larger number of guesses across more machines, the attacker can increase their chances of correctly guessing the password without locking out the account or alerting administrators. A good event management system would notice the sudden high level of guesses across all systems and alert administrators about the extremely abnormal event. A few mistyped passwords every few minutes on a network are usually expected events, but thousands of badly guessed passwords in one minute would usually be indicative of a malicious event (or a runaway application, which is just as important).

Alerting

Where event log management systems show their real value is in how well they filter the unneeded noise and alert on useful actionable events. Critical event messages should always lead to an immediate alert and a responsive investigation. As previously mentioned, an event record should be defined as actionable when the event record indicates a strong likelihood of malicious activity, excessive (sustained) system activity, an unexpected (sustained) drop in system activity, or mission-critical application performance issues or failure.

A good event log management system should come predefined with common alerts (such as excessive account lockouts) and allow administrators to create their own alerts for specific events (deviations from expected baselines that exceed a certain threshold). Sometimes it might take multiple correlated event messages from multiple systems to generate an alert. Other times, depending on the event message's rarity, a single event message (e.g., logon to a fake "trap" account) would be enough to generate an alert. A good system comes with predefined alerts for the event messages most administrators would want to be alerted to and enough filters to slough away the junk.

Alerting should allow a variety of different methods to contact the administrator or incident response team. Certainly, every event management system should allow email contacts, SMS messages, paging, and SNMP traps. The best allow interfacing to other monitoring systems, like help desk systems, so that the alert and incident response can be formally tracked.

As a side note, every good alerting system has throttling built in. Throttling allows multiple instances of the same already alerted upon message instance to be sent just once. For example, suppose an alert was configured to send a cellphone text message if a port scan was attempted against a server. Throttling would prevent multiple port scans from generating hundreds or thousands of texts if they originated from the same malicious attempt.

Reporting
Lastly, event metrics should be used for relevant event logging categories, including security, auditing and compliance, systems monitoring, and application tuning and troubleshooting.

Reporting can simply declare aggregated statistics or the number of alerts received in a particular area. If event management is done right, the collected events lead to a reduction in the events that set off the alerts. Reporting metrics allow management to report on improvements over time, and improvements indicate money and resources well spent.

After all the planning and testing, make sure to document every part of your event log management plan. Be sure to include the people, processes, and systems necessary to consistently apply and enforce your event management plan.

Event Log Management Program
First, document the goals of your event log management program. Security alerting, compliance, systems management, and/or application tuning and troubleshooting—which of those log uses are included in your goals?

Second, decide what devices and computers need to be monitored to comply with your stated goals. What log event messages need to be generated to meet the goals? This is tough, although vendors and regulatory bodies are more likely today to have specific recommendations than in the past. Many event log management system vendors come with settings to monitor for predefined events for a particular type of goal.

Third, decide how, where, and at what intervals you'll collect the logs. Will event messages be left locally, collected at branch nodes, and then forwarded, or will they be collected to a central database? Make a decision that balances the optimization of the event log management system with the service-level requirements of the network.

Fourth, decide which collected event messages will become actionable events and which will simply end up on reports or stored in databases. If your event log strategy ends up generating more noise than useful events, go back and refine your policy. When appropriately configured, it should warn you of actionable events and automatically filter the noise.

Consider outsourcing the whole thing if you don't have the time, equipment, expertise, or software to handle it yourself. There are dozens of excellent software and service companies that can take you from having no log analysis to having top-notch log analysis in a short time.

The idea is to create a nearly self-managing event log system, where only the aberrant events get turned into action items to be investigated. Sure, plenty of those investigated items will turn out to be legitimate (or technically misbehaving) events, but you will have another great tool in your arsenal and become that proactive IT department you've always wanted be.

Readers are again encouraged to download and read NIST's Special Publication 800-92 (https://csrc.nist.gov/publications/detail/sp/800-92/final) for more details behind each log management lifecycle phase.

> Note: Some of the text of this section was taken from my previously published work in *InfoWorld*'s "Log Analysis Deep Dive Report".

Chapter 7 examined the traits of good data to drive a better Data-Driven Computer Defense plan. Chapter 8, "The Data-Driven Computer Defense Lifecycle", discusses how a DDD plan fits in your organization's overall defenses and the cycle of creating and improving your data-driven defense plan.

8 The Data-Driven Computer Defense Lifecycle

Chapter 8 examines the Data-Driven Computer Defense lifecycle and discusses other defense-in-depth defenses that should be included.

"I know of no more encouraging fact than the unquestionable ability of man to elevate his life by a conscious endeavor."—Henry David Thoreau

Recap

As summarized in the figure below, a Data-Driven Computer Defense uses data-driven analysis to better identify the most damaging current and future most likely successful threats and uses them to more efficiently align mitigations.

A data-driven analysis leads to a data-driven streamlined response.

Alignment Principle:
A key goal of an implemented data-driven computer security defense is to more directly align and funnel mitigations against the root-causes of the most successful threats

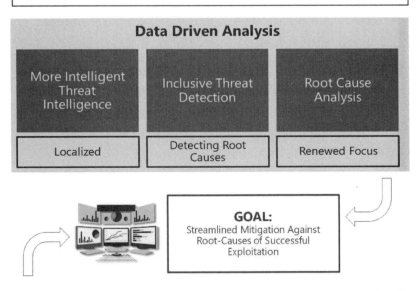

Data Driven Analysis

More Intelligent Threat Intelligence	Inclusive Threat Detection	Root Cause Analysis
Localized	Detecting Root Causes	Renewed Focus

GOAL:
Streamlined Mitigation Against Root-Causes of Successful Exploitation

Data Driven Response

Better Risk Treatment	Implement Risk-Aligned Mitigation	Measurable Accountable Outcomes
Tied to Root Causes	Aligned to Biggest Threats	Are Defenses Successful?

Instead of expending energy on remote and less likely to be successful threats, defensive efficiency is improved by focusing on local threat intelligence data, root causes of initial exploitation (e.g. unpatched software, social engineering, etc.), and improving threat detection through gap analysis review. These steps help defenders make a better risk assessment for each individual threat, compare the risk of different threats against each other, and identify the most likely damaging successful threats. After choosing which threats to focus on, data-driven defenders can better apply the right mitigations in the right places in the right amounts at the right time to achieve measurably lower risk and accountable outcomes. This results in more efficient mitigations against the top threats and root causes (as shown in the figure below).

Risk-ranked threat perception leads to risk-ranked defenses

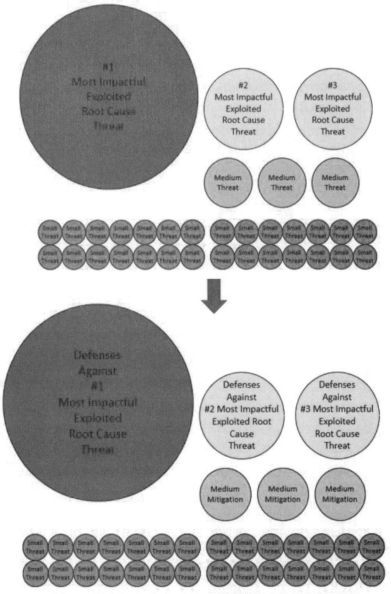

May decide that the cost of defending against small threats is not a good business decision

In order for the complete benefits of a data-driven defense to be fully recognized, it has to become part of the organization's culture and be broadly implemented.

The Data-Driven Computer Defense Lifecycle

A Data-Driven Computer Defense has a lifecycle (summarized below), beginning with collecting better threat intelligence, ending by holding existing mitigations accountable against expectations, and then starting the process all over again.

The Data-Driven Computer Defense lifecycle

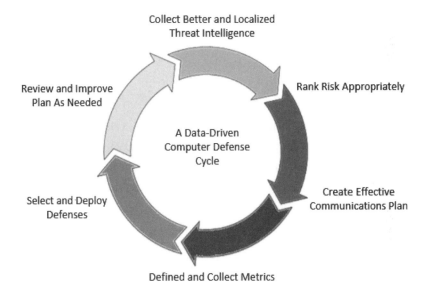

Let's explore each stage of the lifecycle further.

Collect Better and Localized Threat Intelligence

Nothing is more important to a computer security defense than the first step of improving threat intelligence. More accurate threat intelligence that focuses on current, local, most successful threats first, followed by the most likely successful future threats, helps better define what the top threats (by damage) are. Improving local threat intelligence and detection is crucial for making an efficient data-driven defense plan.

Rank Risks Appropriately

Once all the biggest threats are known, they can be more clearly ranked against each other. You're going to give less emphasis to the old way of ranking threats by blindly accepting a vendor's pronouncement that a particular threat is a "high priority". Instead, you're going to use the improved threat intelligence of your own organization's experience to drive your ranked threat list.

Create an Effective Communications Plan

Once all the top threats are known and ranked, they should be communicated across the organization, in accordance with their actual local risk. In most cases, you'll have a number one top threat, perhaps followed by one, two, or a handful of other big threats. These are usually followed by dozens of threats that all together don't usually account for the risk accumulated by one of the top threats.

You need to clearly communicate what the top threats are to each group in the organization, according to the level of detail and strategy needed for each group. For example, the CEO will have one level, and the CIO and the CSO will have another. Those positions want to hear about your long-term strategy for how you are dealing with the top threats, along with compliance issues, money, resources, and other C-level concerns. A front-line employee, not in the IT department, probably needs less strategic detail and more education about how the threat will be impacting their position specifically (e.g. technical defenses coming their way or new education, etc.)

and how they can help. An effective communications plan gives the right education in the right places, all focused on eliminating top threats.

Define and Collect Metrics

Once the top threats are identified, everyone across the organization should come together to identify potential metrics and discuss how to collect them or make existing ones more accurate (if needed). Metrics help drive the well-oiled machine that is a Data-Driven Computer Defense. Gut feelings and experience are backed up or replaced by good data. The mantra for this component should be "If you can't measure it, you can't do it."

Select and Deploy Root Cause Defenses

A Data-Driven Computer Defense plan focuses on root causes (e.g. unpatched software, social engineering, misconfiguration, human errors, etc.) to create mitigations. You cannot defeat a car thief by worrying about the brakes after the car is stolen. You cannot defeat malware by worrying solely about the accuracy of your antivirus software, which will never be perfect. Every threat uses a root cause exploit method to break into an organization. Only be reducing root causes will you reduce the threats. Stop one malware program, and you stop one malware program. Stop one root cause exploit avenue, and you stop every malware program (and hacker) that might otherwise have used that root cause to be successful.

Review and Improve the Plan as Needed

The entire Data-Driven Computer Defense process is a cyclical journey from start to finish and back again. At its core, it's a moving, constantly changing plan, much like the threats it is trying to minimize. The key question at any given point in the cycle is "Are there any deficiencies that need to be improved?"

You can begin that process by asking the following questions:

- Is threat intelligence accurate about the top current and future most likely SUCCESSFUL threats?
- Is threat detection of the top threats accurate? Are there too many false-negatives or false-positives? Are there some top threats that you are missing altogether?
- Are emerging threats being seen and dealt with faster?
- Are root causes being identified and acted upon?
- Are communications focusing on the right things and communicating them across the organization? Can all employees name the top successful threats?
- Are the right mitigations being applied, and how do they succeed?

These questions should be asked all the time, and at the very least they should be formally addressed and documented once per quarter. Significant deficiencies should be discussed and rectified, if possible, and be cost-effective.

The Perfect Data-Driven Computer Defense

In a perfect world where a data-driven defense is pushed to its fullest efficiency, as much of the process would be automated as possible. Data analytics would be used to process local threat intelligence, which would drive automatic risk ranking. Relative risk rankings, along with artificial intelligence (AI), would drive defenses and help create communication plans. Results in the deployed defenses would be used to drive the next cycle of reviews. Any product or service that helps you to automate a part of the data-driven defense lifecycle should be given serious consideration.

Defense-in-Depth

A Data-Driven Computer Defense does not mean you stop doing all the other defense-in-depth things (such as credential hygiene, the Security Development Lifecycle, improved authentication, "Assume Breach" defenses, etc.) that are necessary for a complete, encompassing, computer security defense. When car manufacturers were working to significantly improve car safety in the 1970s and 1980s, it didn't mean that traffic safety stopped being improved.

To be clear, with a data-driven defense you absolutely need to focus on doing the right things in the right amounts first and then doing everything else. A data-driven defense attempts to stop people from focusing on all the other stuff first to the exclusion of the biggest, most successful threats and best mitigations. A data-driven defense means you don't concentrate on implementing smartcards when you should instead focus on badly patched software or anti–social-engineering training, but that doesn't mean that you altogether ignore smartcards as a part of a good computer security defense, particularly if they can help reduce a significant root exploit cause.

Part of the Big Picture

A Data-Driven Computer Defense is a conceptual framework and methodology for helping to more efficiently align mitigations against the top threats. Although I believe a data-driven defense plan's key focus is revolutionary, the general processes it follows are not. There are many computer security frameworks, each with similarities and differences, but they are all focused on trying to minimize cybersecurity risk.

For example, the NIST Framework for Improving Critical Infrastructure Cybersecurity (https://www.nist.gov/sites/default/files/documents/cyberframework/cybersecurity-framework-021214.pdf) components, summarized in the figure below, map fairly consistently to the data-driven defense approach.

The NIST cybersecurity framework components

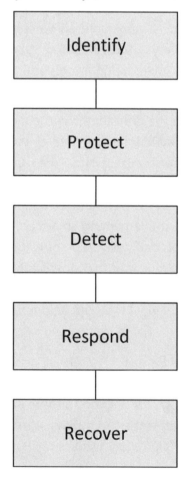

The last two components, *Respond* and *Recover*, refer more to traditional incident response and minimizing resulting damages, which a data-driven defense plan does not cover. This doesn't mean an organization should not include those components in their overall risk framework. It just means it's not something that a Data-Driven Computer Defense plan specifically focuses on because those components are already well covered and agreed upon by most computer security practitioners. Use a data-driven defense plan to better perform the three first NIST framework components, *Identify*, *Detect*, and *Protect*.

> Note: If you're interested in additional, more inclusive IT governance and operational frameworks (more than just cybersecurity), check out ISACA's COBIT (http://www.isaca.org/COBIT/Pages/default.aspx), ISO/IEC 27001: 2013 (https://en.wikipedia.org/wiki/ISO/IEC_27001:2013), or Information Technology Infrastructure Library (ITIL) (https://en.wikipedia.org/wiki/ITIL).

Four Computer Security Defense Pillars

A Data-Driven Computer Defense uses local experiences and data to drive all the defenses and responses. The overall defense memes can be broken down into four defense pillars (shown below).

The four computer security defense pillars

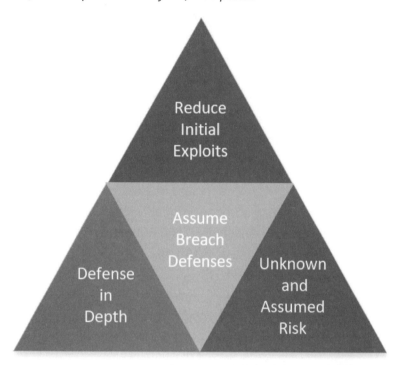

As discussed throughout this book, a computer data-driven defense focuses on exploit root causes and does this specifically to prevent initial breaches. If you can't stop the initial breach, then you will never significantly minimize risk to the organization.

Use Assume Breach Defenses

Right now, most organizations are so porous that they must assume that they are either currently breached by hackers or malware or easily could be. This is the case with 99.999% of organizations not disconnected from the Internet and not running on a classified network. There is occasionally hacking of organizations that are disconnected from the Internet and running on classified networks, but it is far less common than hacking of organizations that are not.

Use the data-driven defense concepts to measure Assume Breach threats and create right-aligned mitigations to assist. For example, if you assume that a hacker can always capture your local administrator password stored on a single computer, you can slow down the attacker's movement in the organization by not using the same administrator password on any other computers. Or you can implement defenses that make it significantly harder for an intruder to retrieve privileged credentials even if they have admin access to a computer (such as is done by Microsoft's Windows 10 Credential Guard™ technology).

While a data-driven defense absolutely wants you to work the hardest on minimizing initial breach exploits, it recognizes that most organizations can't prevent them 100%, and so a data-driven defense must be done inside and out. You want to try to prevent intruders from getting inside your networks and slow them down if they do get inside.

Most defenders are already operating this way, and just because they deploy very strong network perimeter firewalls doesn't mean they leave a "soft, chewy center" for any attacker or malware that makes it past the perimeter defenses. Instead, use an Assume Breach defense until you can use data to show that it isn't something your organization needs to worry about anymore (and if so, congratulations!). Use Data-Driven Computer Defense concepts for both initial and subsequent malicious actions.

Individual Defense-in-Depth Recommendations

. There are dozens of defense-in-depth models and recommendations for what we all should be concentrating on. The biggest difference between them and the data-driven defense plan promoted in this book is that they often base their recommendations on a society's global experience and recommendations for success, while a data-driven defense plan says that it is best to first use your organization's local, most timely experience.

This doesn't mean the other models have no value. It just means that you should take them for what they are, global recommendations without any idea of what your local, biggest, successful threats are. They have no idea what your defenses are, what your organization already defends well against, and where the gaps are.

If you do not have any data of local experiences, you can start with any of the popular defense-in-depth recommendations from highly respected organizations. Here are some respected and popular recommendations:

<u>General Security Control Recommendations</u>
- Center for Internet Security Top 20 CIS Controls™ (formerly known as the SANS Top 20) (https://www.cisecurity.org/controls/)
- OWASP Top 10: The Ten Most Critical Web Application Security Risks (https://www.owasp.org/images/7/72/OWASP_Top_10-2017_%28en%29.pdf.pdf)
- U.S. Department of Homeland Security Continuous Diagnostics and Mitigation (https://www.dhs.gov/cdm)

- NIST Special Publication 800-53, "Security and Privacy Controls for Federal Information Systems and Organizations" (http://nvlpubs.nist.gov/nistpubs/SpecialPublications/NIST.SP.800-53r4.pdf)

Specific, Detailed Configuration Controls
- Defense Information Systems Agency, or DISA (http://disa.mil/Cybersecurity/Secure-Configuration-Guidance)
- U.S. Government Configuration Baseline, or USGCB, (https://csrc.nist.gov/Projects/United-States-Government-Configuration-Baseline)
- Center for Internet Security CIS Benchmarks™ baselines (https://www.cisecurity.org/cis-benchmarks/)
- Microsoft Windows Security Baselines (https://docs.microsoft.com/en-us/windows/device-security/windows-security-baselines)

A Data-Driven Computer Defense is easy to map to these other control frameworks and specific configuration recommendations.

Focus, Focus, Focus

As much as I like the frameworks and best practice recommendations discussed in the previous section, the key missing distinction with them is focus. We already know that the vast majority of risk to most organizations is from social engineering and unpatched software. These other recommendations often mention these two top-tier threats, but they don't stress the true importance of doing them well. The average framework document mentioned in the previous section runs from 80 to 100 pages. But the text devoted to patching software and providing security awareness training is probably 5 to 20 sentences. At the same time, items that deal with far less real-world risk have many pages devoted to them. These documents are good, but they treat all threats either equally or disproportionately to actual risk (like bubbles in a glass of champagne).

Additionally, even when these documents cover the most important mitigations, such as patch management and security awareness training, they don't go into very much detail. They say something like "Make sure to patch all critical vulnerabilities in a timely manner." Although that is a good philosophy to follow, it treats all critical vulnerabilities as having equal weight in mitigating risk, and we know from Chapter 5, "A DDD Example", that not all patches are alike.

Every recommended mitigation must be scrutinized to determine which ones have the best chance of diminishing the most risk the fastest. Use and follow respected organizations' frameworks and guidelines, but implement their best practice recommendations in a way that ensures you get the best bang for your buck in reducing risk first.

My Personal Top Defense Recommendations

I've been a computer security consultant for over 30 years, and my clients are among the most secure out there, not only because they follow a data-driven defense, but because I have long been pushing what is THE best bang-for-the-computer-security-defense-buck. Even though every client is different, most share many common issues. Here is the list of the most common computer security defense recommendations I give on a regular basis:

- Improve anti–social-engineering training.

- Improve patch management, focusing first on the applications most exploited in your organization.
- Admins should always use secure admin workstations with very strong security controls, including not allowing access to or from the Internet. See https://msdn.microsoft.com/en-us/library/mt186538.aspx for more details.
- Implement Assume Breach defenses, like preventing privileged credential theft.
- Improve monitoring and alerting.
- Use honeypots. Honeypots are "fake" computers and devices that exist only to detect and alert on anomalous activity.
- Minimize or eliminate permanent elevated group membership. Instead use "just-in-time" and "just-enough" mechanisms.
- Use smartcards and/or two-factor authentications. (It's hard for hackers to steal passwords when you don't have them.)
- Implement "always on" encryption for both storage and transferring data.
- Use application control "whitelisting".
- Use a secure OS following the vendor's best practice recommendations.
- For the serious security professional, use Qubes OS (https://www.qubes-os.org/) or something like it.
- If you write or develop software, use the Security Development Lifecycle or something similar to decrease security bugs.
- Save all critical data to a secure, less hackable location, like offline storage.

If you don't see one or two of your favorite recommendations, like firewalls or antivirus software, it might be because I just don't see them as top, necessary defenses. Or I might have overlooked one when I was writing this book. If you feel I have missed one, send it to me at roger@banneretcs.com, and if I agree, I might possibly add it to the next edition of the book.

A data-driven defense has a lifecycle starting from better threat intelligence and ending with properly aligned, accountable mitigations, which are frequently reviewed. A Data-Driven Computer Defense plan is part of a larger IT security framework, which is part of a larger IT governance framework. Chapter 9 examines more Data-Driven Computer Defense implementation examples.

9 More Implementation Examples

Moving to a Data-Driven Computer Defense can only be accomplished on a case-by-case basis. Every organization is different and has a different starting point. Chapter 9 highlights many Data-Driven Computer Defense examples that have been used by some of the world's largest organizations and can be used to spearhead your new projects.

> *"In theory, there is no difference between theory and practice. In practice, there is."*—First appeared in print in the 1986 book *Pascal: An Introduction to the Art and Science of Programming* by Walter J. Savitch

Moving to a Data-Driven Defense

In an existing organization, it is difficult to move wholesale from a non-data-driven defense to a Data-Driven Computer Defense in a single step. Moving to a data-driven defense usually requires adopting data-driven tenets on a case-by-case, project-by-project basis, starting with the easiest opportunities. Implementers should begin by picking "proof-of-concept" (POC) projects where the data-driven concepts are easy to execute, the data and metrics can be gathered more easily, and the benefits are more readily seen. The summaries in the following sections describe real-life deployments of Data-Driven Computer Defense concepts.

The Microsoft Backstreet Project

I was working in India as a Microsoft employee teaching a Windows Vista computer security class to other Microsoft employees. During my first day of classes, an IT security employee came in and announced that he had to check each of the class computers for the Conficker malware program (https://en.wikipedia.org/wiki/Conficker).

He had a USB key drive with an antivirus program that he could plug in, and it would automatically run. There were about 50 computers in the classroom, and every computer he tested was infected with Conficker. As he got to about the twentieth computer in a row that was infected, I asked to see his USB key. I disabled the autorun functionality on my computer, plugged in his USB key, and ran my antivirus on the plugged-in drive. Sure enough, it was infected. The IT security employee had unknowingly infected his USB drive on one of the former computers, and he now subsequently infected every single computer that he plugged the USB drive into. It was a self-fulfilling prophecy.

For those defenders who had to fight the Conficker worm, it was one of the hardest malware programs to fully eradicate from any corporate environment. It would go from one or two computers to many more, and you would find infected USB key drives for years. It disabled automated backups (making it harder to recover from), caused network slowness, locked out user accounts, disabled services, stopped antivirus programs from working, and prevented Microsoft patches from being downloaded.

Conficker first appeared in November 2008 and ended up infecting tens of millions of computers over many years. It spread using at least three different exploit vectors, including exploiting a patched Windows vulnerability (MS08-067), password guessing against weakly password-protected NETBIOS drive shares (using a list of 100 very simple but common passwords), and exploiting the USB autorun modality. It went from being just a nuisance to causing significant operational issues for many organizations. It would die down in popularity only to reemerge and start to spread again.

Right from the start, Microsoft told customers what to do to avoid getting infected and what to do if they got infected. Microsoft aggressively made sure that everyone had the MS08-067 patch applied. They co-founded an industry working group to study and eradicate Conficker. Microsoft even announced an unprecedented reward of $250,000 for information leading to the malware author's identification and arrest (although I think that went unawarded). Still, no matter what they did, Conficker continued to spread.

Finally, with a project internally called Backstreet, Microsoft decided to take a more data-driven approach to Conficker. Because Microsoft customers download hundreds of millions of patches each month, Microsoft's patch install routine had the telemetry ability to check each participating computer for Conficker and also for each of the three possible Conficker vulnerabilities. The data was reported back to Microsoft and the Backstreet project.

To the project leader's surprise, the USB key autorun method was the most popular attack vector, and not the missing patch as most had previously assumed. It was amazing to some that a method that required more human intervention in order to succeed was infecting more computers than missing patches or weak passwords, which were automated methods that worked over a network.

Given this new data, Microsoft, decided to take a fairly drastic step and disable autorun from running on removable media drives by default. This was a pretty big deal at the time. It was going to remove a decades-old default behavior that users loved for its convenience. This doesn't happen all that often in computer security, especially when the result risks making hundreds of millions of customers unhappy. Obviously, Microsoft decided that the people upset with the ongoing Conficker disruptions were going to outnumber the people upset about the disabling of autorun. It only takes a few more clicks to run waiting media, but it can take hours to clean a Conficker infection.

In April 2009, Microsoft decided to modify the forthcoming beta version of Microsoft Windows 7 so that autorun was turned off by default on removable media. Microsoft expected that this would make Windows 7 significantly less likely to be infected by Conficker, and after a few months, the collected data confirmed the theory.

Initially, Microsoft didn't want to force older versions of their OS (i.e. Microsoft Windows XP™ and Microsoft Windows Vista™) to have changed functionality, but Conficker was still a huge problem on those platforms. So, in February 2011, Microsoft sent out a new patch to all customers downloading the free monthly Microsoft patches (in the Windows Update program) that disabled the autorun feature when dealing with removable media. Microsoft did publish ways for admins and users to bypass the autorun patch, although the disabling of autoruns would become the default behavior if the user or admin did nothing to stop it.

After the patch downloaded and ran across hundreds of millions of XP and Vista machines, Conficker's infection rate immediately plummeted from many millions per month to maybe a few hundred thousand. From that point forward, not only did Conficker continue to decrease in popularity, but so too did any malware program that used the USB autorun vector (and, due to Conficker's success, there were quite a few malware programs exploiting USB autorun by that time).

I wasn't a part of the Microsoft Backstreet Conficker eradication team, but I knew about it and, along with a few other employees, really took to heart what data analytics could mean to computer security. It was the genesis of what became my Data-Driven Computer Defense philosophy. I figured if such an approach worked across one malware program and all the others like it, why couldn't it work on all defenses? It turns out that it can.

After a few more intermediate experiments, I began my life's work dedicated to a Data-Driven Computer Defense. Wherever I could, I espoused the data-driven computer defense philosophy and implemented it as much as possible. Rarely would a company allow me to do a full implementation. Most of the time I had to prove the data-driven defense concept by starting with more limited POC projects. As the smaller POCs proved successful, I was allowed to do larger and larger projects. Whether they were small or large projects, they all shared one thing in common: If the questions were right and the data was good, they significantly reduced risk. You, too, will likely start with more limited POC examples.

Data-Driven Examples

The following sections provide some more data-driven defense examples to gain inspiration from or adapt to your needs.

Mean-Time-to-Detect

Most organizations are happy enough with antivirus reports summarizing how many malware programs were detected and removed by their antivirus software in a given time period. But that metric doesn't mean anything super useful about the increase or decrease in malware risk over time. A detected and removed malware program is no risk to the environment. Accuracy and detection speed are more important.

If an antivirus program detects malware at the same instant that it is trying to enter a computer, that's an example of the antivirus software completely eliminating the risk. The problem is that no stand-alone antivirus software that I'm aware of has a report telling you how long it took from the time the malware program first appeared on the computer until the antivirus program detected and removed it. The antivirus vendor probably sees no benefit to its own interests in providing such information.

The time that it took for the antivirus program to detect the malware program after the malware entered the computer is the most real risk (i.e. mean-time-to-detect). During that time, the malware program can do anything it was designed to do, limited only by the security context the malware program is running under.

> Note: How long a malware program or hacker is actively exploiting something before detection and removal is known as *"dwell time"*.

In a very large company, we designed a scheme to figure out the mean-time-to-detect for every malware program across every computer. All the computers already had a running application control whitelisting program, which in this case was Microsoft AppLocker™ in audit-only mode. This meant that it was silently recording any newly installed or executed program that differed from each computer's original baseline configuration. The users of this company didn't even know that AppLocker was running. It simply logged newly appearing programs in the Windows event log and did nothing else.

We decided that every time the antivirus software detected and removed a malware program, we would look to see when the malware program first installed or executed. We did this by always extracting all AppLocker and antivirus log event messages to a database while extracting only the minimum needed log event message details to get an accurate answer.

We started on a limited, proof-of-concept basis and quickly moved it to a full-scale rollout. In a very short time after setting up this data-driven metric, we had lots of useful data. The vast majority of malware was getting detected and removed before it was executed. This was great news. There were, however, times when it took up to three days for the antivirus program to detect and remove particular malware family classes. We were able to take our data to the antivirus vendor and ask why it was taking longer for certain malware classes. The vendor responded, giving us good technical answers for why we were seeing what we were seeing, but at the same time we noticed that even these malware family classes started to be detected faster over time. The vendor had apparently made some changes that decreased the mean-time-to-detect.

The project was a huge success. Not only did it measure the organization's mean-time-to-detect risk over time, and we could see it dropping, but it also helped with other computer security activities.

Hosts Also Determine Risk

Most vulnerability reports list vulnerabilities as high-, medium-, or low-risk threats regardless of the type of computer they get exploited on. But the computer an exploit lands on has a big impact on the amount of overall risk to the organization. If the same exploit or malware program is on the CEO's computer or a public kiosk computer, that creates different types and amounts of risk. Using a data-driven defense, you can assign different levels of risk to different computers and let that data impact the rest of the risk calculation and defense.

The same organization mentioned in the previous example classified many computers and users as critical risks, meaning that compromises of their computer or software could lead to significantly elevated risk to the organization. The critical-risk systems included critical application software, supporting network devices, infrastructure servers (e.g. DNS, DHCP, etc.), and people who were administrators on critical software systems, payroll and accounts receivable software, as examples. All-in-all, more than 15,000 employees (out of over 200,000) and their computers and devices were classified as being a critical risk. The company also identified over 100 critical "line-of-business" software programs that ran the business.

When a device ranked as a critical risk became infected with malware, if the company's mean-time-to-detect was more than 20 seconds, they sent the operator an automated email explaining the issue and risk, gave details, and asked them to self-report if they felt that they were compromised while processing secrets (e.g. data or logon credential) or viewing confidential data. Although they started with a 20 second baseline, that was eventually changed to 60 seconds and then 120 seconds because of timing issues that created some false-positives and a reevaluation of the real risk in such a short time period.

The idea is that not all computers, users, and devices are the same risk to the organization, and so they should not be treated the same. Malware that goes undetected for days on a database server or the CFO's computer represents more potential risk than if it went undetected on a stand-alone cafeteria computer.

Similarly, if malware was found on some super-critical computers involved in sensitive operations, regardless of the mean-time-to-detect value, the server was automatically cut off from the network and an emergency forensic response investigation was ordered. For example, if a pass-the-hash toolkit was found on a domain controller or the CEO's computer, the organization didn't care if it was removed instantaneously. Its mere presence was enough to initiate a stronger, more immediate response.

All that was needed for these host rating scenarios was a single criticality rating saved to an already existing inventory database for all users, computers, devices, and software. Then when malware was detected and removed, the records from the inventory program were used to indicate host criticality, which then could be used to initiate a particular response. An organization's *identify-detect-respond* processes should reflect that understanding. Does your antivirus detection software and

201

related data help you prioritize risk according to device, software, and user?

Using Inventory to Calculate Risk

Many organizations I consult with about a data-driven defense love the theory, but they tell me their organization is nowhere near mature enough to begin to implement it. As I've stated in previous chapters, figuring out your biggest risks and their root causes is the beginning point for the rest of the data-driven defense lifecycle. Many organizations tell me that they wish they had some useful data to begin testing data-driven concepts on. I often respond by asking them if they have an accurate software and hardware inventory. I've never met an organization that didn't. With that you can do a lot.

Take every computer that was detected as having malware and compare it to its hardware and software inventory, in aggregate. You want to look for trends that indicate higher or lower exploitation rates for particular hardware or software configurations. Here are some sample questions to answer:

- What hardware and software configurations are exploited the most (percentage-wise)? Which are exploited the least?

- What departments are exploited the most and the least? What are their locations?

- What browser and version are running when most computers are or aren't infected?

- What day of the week or time of day are the most people's devices or software infected?

- What day of the week or time do most people type in the wrong logon information?

- If you have mean-time-to-detect information, what hardware and software computer configurations make the best and worst times?

With just two data sets that likely already exist in your organization, you will be able to point out software and hardware attributes that were more or less prevalent on computers that were compromised versus not compromised, and you can use that data to try to determine risk and additional mitigations.

For example, it's common to see substantially more exploitations on computers with the following attributes:

- Unpatched software, especially unpatched Internet browser add-on software. But what software? What versions?

- Older operating system versions.

- Older browser versions.

- 32-bit systems (versus 64-bit systems).

- Systems running non-current versions of anti-malware software or none at all.

- Higher exploitation percentages (in particular geographic regions throughout the world).

- Non-domain joined computers.

- User Account Control (UAC) is disabled.

Microsoft frequently reports these types of statistics for global Microsoft customers in their quarterly Security Intelligence Reports (http://www.microsoft.com/sir). The information is usually shown by Windows operating system version and often by country or region.

An organization can compare its own software and hardware inventory to its own rates of exploitation to determine what device traits seem to lead to higher risk. For example, one browser version or another may lead to more exploitations, or perhaps risk can be lowered by moving from 32-bit to 64-bit systems.

Newer, more up-to-date hardware and software usually means fewer exploitations (although not always). If this is true when you're analyzing your own data and you can put a dollar value on the average exploit recovery event, you might be able to argue, with the data to back you up, that moving everyone to a newer computer or software version will be cheaper in the long run.

With a good inventory and detection of successful exploitations, any organization should be able to determine relative risks for different software and hardware configurations.

Root Cause Report

A Data-Driven Computer Defense plan includes focusing on root causes of initial exploitations. Minimize root causes, and you kill entire classes of malware and hackers.

One company I worked for understood this better than most. They didn't initially collect or store any root cause data. After my data-driven defense presentation, they did gap analysis and changed many of their processes and tools to better account for root causes.

In some cases, they realized that their software and methodologies were already tracking root causes, and they just had to look for the data. In other cases, they had to buy new software that had the explicit ability to look for and document root causes.

One quick method to generate a lot of root cause data to compare the top malware programs detected by your anti-malware program against the most likely root causes of those malware programs. First, generate a report listing the most popular malware programs detected in your environment and pull those results to a small database or spreadsheet. Next, research the most common ways that those programs can exploit a computer.

Most malware programs only exploit using one or a few predefined exploitation methods. For instance, most malware exploiting across the web comes from "web exploitation kits" (https://www.f-secure.com/en/web/labs_global/exploit-kits), which are predefined to check for and use a few specific exploits. For example, some exploitation kits only look for a few Microsoft vulnerabilities. Others only work with particular browsers and their plug-ins, such as Java, Adobe Acrobat Reader, and Flash. In the database with the top found malware programs, add a cross-tab section that lists all the possible ways the malware could have broken in, if defined. Then you can run a report to list the top root cause methods for the top found malware programs.

The company discussed in this section developed an employee interview process where, after any malware was detected on an employee's computer, they asked the employee how they thought it might have been infected. At first, the company collected data by just emailing or calling the employee and asking the question. This transitioned to an automated email that was sent as part of the detection report process. The interview process was promoted as part of a larger employee awareness campaign. They went from collecting no data on root causes to collecting gobs of it.

From there they were able to create a report that revealed how much overall exploit damage could be avoided by completely fixing a particular root cause. (A simplified example is shown in the table below.)

Defensive Mitigation	% of Threats Mitigated by Defense
Better social engineering training against email phishing attacks	94%
Better patch management of two software programs	52%
Two-factor authentication	35%
Longer and more complex passwords	2%

Note: % of Threats Mitigated by Defense will often add up to more than 100%, as several defenses will often mitigate the same threats.

They also calculated how much it would cost them to minimize the root causes, so they could say something similar to "For $98,000 in additional cost to better patch two programs, we can expect to remove $198,000 in resulting exploitation damage." And so on.

Their goal was to directly identify how much of their current threats would be removed by applying particular and specific mitigations and attach costs to both the problem and the potential remedies. The example above is a simplified representation of a table used in the real production environment, but the concept is the same. When you can collect better data, you can better assign risk and costs to mitigate.

Data-Driven Security Awareness Training

Security Awareness Training is getting better, although not enough companies are using it or using enough of it, if you look at the data and how often social engineering is involved in doing significant damage to an organization. Companies should review the most damaging social engineering techniques against their company and then create or buy targeted, quality, end-user education (and products) to fight it.

I don't have a preference of whether the end-user training is created internally or purchased externally as long as it is targeted to the most damaging types of social engineering and is quality education that excels at accomplishing its objectives.

Working with External Education Companies

External end-user education companies, like KnowBe4 (https://www.knowbe4.com/), offer a wide variety of commercial quality end-user training services. If you select an external company, select products that most closely match your organization's specific biggest threats. The vendor may already have something available that matches exactly what you need, or you can work with them to create custom, more targeted, courses. Whether your training is made internally or externally, the data-driven key is to use your own local data and experience to determine exactly what type of training should result in the biggest decrease in risk to your organization.

Simulated "Fake" Email Phishing Campaigns
Email phishing is a huge problem in most organizations. A
growing number of companies now regularly conduct
simulated ("fake" phishing) email test campaigns against their
employees on a regular basis. Test phishing campaigns are a
GREAT way to educate the end-user masses about the
techniques and risks of email-based phishing attacks. The fake
phishing campaigns should match as closely as possible the
real-life phishing campaigns that have been most damaging to
your company. KnowBe4's long-term data shows that most
organizations can take their users' "phish prone" rate from
about 30% to 2% with a combination of security awareness
training and simulated phishing test campaigns
(https://info.knowbe4.com/2018-phishing-by-industry-
benchmarking-report).

These simulated phishing campaigns are great ways to collect
data on which users, groups, and locations are more
susceptible to email phishing, and then use that data to provide
education specifically to those people. Companies like
KnowBe4 make the follow-up education an automatic part of
the campaign. Just make sure the education is targeted
specifically to your organization's needs. Data-driven defenders
should also look for opportunities to see up or down trends for
groups of users and try to find out what is or isn't working, and
why.

Spearphishing-Education Example
Social engineering encompasses more than just email phishing.
It also includes web site-based phishing attacks, instant
messaging spam, tech support scams, physical presence hacks,
phone call cons, CEO wire fraud, swatting attacks, and
essentially any medium that allows unauthenticated content. A

data-driven defense enumerates the top social engineering threats that are currently being the most successful against your organization and the most likely future ones, and it trains employees against those.

One company I worked with had experienced multiple advanced persistent threat (APT) spearphishing attacks that had resulted in the loss of intellectual property and partial reputation damage. They responded by requiring every employee to take 30 minutes of generic social-engineering training each year. But it did not work effectively enough to significantly reduce the success of phishing against the company.

So, they started to test different types of training and compare the success of one type versus another over time. They found out one type of training seemed to have the most success and another type, for reasons that are still unknown, seemed to actually increase the odds of someone falling for a social engineering attack. They got rid of that latter training class.

The training that they kept and pushed out to the rest of the company was a highly personal and customized anti-spearphishing training video (created using an external training company) that shared the true story of a well-known, well-liked, very smart, prominent co-worker who had been successfully spearphished. He narrated the video detailing what he was doing (i.e. working on the weekend) when he received an unexpected email from "a co-worker". The email referenced a confidential project they were both working on and instructed the employee to click on an encrypted PDF document to see something similar to their project that one of their competitors was working on. The victim wasn't expecting the email, and it purportedly came from the sender's personal account, which was not normal, but it referenced information "only the sender" could know. With that, he clicked on the link and accidentally infected his computer.

The respected co-worker even shared how even though he was fairly sure he had just been successfully spearphished, he was embarrassed to call the company's help desk right away to report the incident. He tried to handle it himself. He didn't call until the next day. When he called, he was surprised to learn that what had happened to him had also happened to other senior leaders and that an incident response team task force had been set up to help recover and protect the company. He shared that his personal embarrassment and the prospect of possibly getting in trouble delayed his calling the help desk. He closed by saying "If it can happen to me, it can happen to anyone. But you can be smarter than me by not opening a strange external email in the first place, calling the purported sender to verify first, and calling the help desk sooner if you think you've been hacked. I regret my slow response, but I'm glad to share my experience here to help others."

The video was a huge hit. The following year, successful spearphishing attacks plummeted. Another data analysis showed that 60 minutes of anti–social-engineering training, instead of just 30 minutes, helped significantly reduce all social engineering risk. Security awareness training is one of the best ways to see a data-driven defense in action and to be able to see measurable results.

Tracking Attacker Histories

A new class of computer security defense now exists that can help any organization better track hacker actions and even proactively notify you when hackers or malware have made it into your environment. It does this by monitoring existing data sources or creating new sources and alerting on anomalous activity.

Some of these products/services track known hacker and malware "command-and-control" centers (usually by IP addresses of known malicious hosts or network segments), and if they find traffic heading out of your internal network to a known hacker site, then they alert you. This is sort of an extension of the spam email "blackhole" methods of yesteryear, where email servers sending spam would be marked as such and all the other email servers would simply stop accepting email from them. Only these new services apply to all network traffic and not just email protocols.

Other companies offer services that are very good at telling you not only that they've detected a malicious action, but also when the malicious origination point first entered your system, where it went, and what it did, in detail, since the beginning of its intrusion until the current time. The graphic information you can get and drill down into is incredible. It's a forensic tracker's dream. I could easily write several chapters about these types of services. They are the epitome of a data-driven defense. And they are everywhere.

I was onsite at a customer's facility one day when the CEO reported that they thought he had been successfully spearphished. The company's security operations center (SOC) quickly brought up a virtual representation of his laptop on a huge console screen. They were quickly able to see the dropped malware program, its name, what it did, what other malicious processes it spawned, and where it moved from there. Very quickly, they could see the same malicious processes existed across over 100 computers and that most instances of them had been created in the last few hours. With a few clicks of the mouse, they froze the malicious processes across all machines, halting more immediate damage. It literally took 10 minutes to see the threat, analyze it in detail, and stop it. Data is an amazing thing.

You, too, can take advantage of such systems. Theoretically, any company should be able to create a similar system within their own company. The logs and data necessary to accomplish similar detection and discovery information exist in nearly every company. All the organization has to do is create a system to aggregate, analyze, and alert on the collected data. Unfortunately, this is usually easier said than done, and for that reason, most companies buy an external vendor's product or service. Either way, whether developed internally or externally, these sorts of malware and hacker detection services and products are great examples of a data-driven defense being used to its best end.

Reprioritizing Criticality Rankings

Nearly all organizations run vulnerability scans on their hosts to ferret out existing vulnerabilities. One company I worked for ran Tenable Nessus™ for general vulnerability scans, Qualys™ for web site vulnerability scanning, HP Fortify™ for code scanning, and a host of other vulnerability analysis tools. Each server and application in their environment had to be completely scanned by each tool before it went live to their production network, and again monthly after that. Nearly every newly scanned server, application, and web site scanned ended up with a list of dozens of found issues to fix. Many computers had over 50 top priority recommendations found (many were repeats for the same issue found in multiple places), and if you believed their risk ranking alone, they all had to be fixed immediately.

You cannot fix 50 "top priorities" all at once. You can only fix a few at most at the same time. This problem begged the question about which of the top issues were really the top issues.

Using data-driven concepts, we analyzed the top current and most likely successful threats against the company, and then we modified each vulnerability scanning tool so that the real top priorities were vulnerabilities that involved those top successful threats. The number one threat was hardcoded authentication secrets (e.g. passwords, private keys, etc.). So, in this company, if your application was found to have hardcoded secrets, fixing that single issue became the number one problem to fix, followed by everything else.

In phase 1 of this project, we modified the vulnerability tools' priority rankings by hand. Most vulnerability scanning tools allowed the admin to set custom priorities. We were able to insert our prioritizations into new fields, which we then indexed and reported out in the vulnerability reports. But the process of updating the custom criticalities in the scanning tools and reporting mechanisms was done manually by hand.

In phase 2 of the project, we automated the reranking of the criticalities, so that when the latest data-driven threat/risk dataset came in to reveal the existing and most likely expected threats, the scan tool criticalities were automatically updated. This project was the epitome of a data-driven defense, and I've since repeated it many times.

Driving SDL Requirements

Companies that create software can reduce risk by training their programmers in Security Development Lifecycle (SDL) practices, requiring the use of SDL-enabling tools, and enforcing SDL requirements. For those interested in more detail on SDL, Microsoft has the most free information and tools dealing with SDL of any company: https://www.microsoft.com/en-us/sdl.

Microsoft has long performed data-driven analysis of the issues and practices that cause the highest number of security bugs in the software that it develops. For example, many years ago, a high percentage of bugs was found to be related to older, legacy, long ago unrecommended programming language features/functions that were known to be very exploitable, such as *strcpy*. Since then, programmers have been trained to avoid using known exploitable programing functions, and Microsoft's code development tools and "security safety checks" explicitly look for them. In Microsoft, it's known as the "banned function calls". See https://msdn.microsoft.com/en-us/library/bb288454.aspx for more details.

Unfortunately, checking for banned code functions after the code is programmed is a little late in the development pathway. Microsoft decided to put in earlier code checks so that coding weaknesses, including banned code functions, would be checked for and blocked at the time the developer tries to "check in" the code into the centralized code repository. No longer would a developer have to wait until someone did a code security review to find those flaws. Now, the developer cannot check it in as delivered code if it has a recognized flaw. This not only finds flaws sooner, but helps incentivize and educate developers faster. It took looking for and collecting data around what was involved in most code bugs in order to automate the process that prevents them.

Individual Personal Behavior Examples

A Data-Driven Computer Defense can be driven at the corporate level, but it can also be done at the individual level, even if not officially recognized by any other corporate structure. The following sections provide some personal real-life examples from my career.

Training

My boss's boss came up to me and asked if I would get involved in a computer security training program that would cover multiple topics using video training. His exact words were "I know you like to do training and education, and we need someone to lead this effort. Will you do it?"

I looked over the list of five training topics and said "Yes." Then I asked which one should be done first? The five topics were completely unrelated and basically looked like a list of pet projects from different senior managers. He said "They are all important. Do whatever one you want to do first."

This, of course, bugged me. I needed data to back the prioritization. The list of topics was wide ranging from social engineering to cloud security. So, I pushed back and said that I wouldn't begin creating the videos until I had a data-driven understanding of which topic needed to be covered the most first.

The organization already had a fairly good understanding of their top threats, using data, and what came back that could improve the organization the most was improved security awareness training followed by improved Security Development Lifecycle (SDL) training.

Having this data motivated not only me, but the entire team that was making the training videos. Nothing helps motivate a team more than feeling like you're all working toward a common goal that will have the greatest possible impact on the company. It motivates even better than money.

Stopping Red Team Attacks

I discussed this in Chapter 6, "Asking the Right Questions", but I'll address it again. I was meeting with a CSO to discuss the benefits of a data-driven defense. He understood the theory, but he wasn't so sure it could be implemented in practice. In frustration, he handed me a recent list of the top 20 ways his red team had broken into his organization's servers. He asked "Which should I do first?" I responded "Exactly!" Without the data we did not know which of the 20 things needed to be done first. But I asked an even better data-driven question: "Which of these things are what the real hackers do the most in your environment?" It's not enough to simply have data, you have to ask the right questions and get the right data.

In the list of 20 things the red team had done, I saw maybe a handful of attack vectors that were common in the real world. Red teams are good at finding vulnerabilities, but a great red team helps you find and fix the vulnerabilities most likely to be accomplished by real-world threats against your company. Who cares if a red team member, with superior knowledge, creates a new zero-day attack to break into something? I'd rather be told of how they captured the crown jewels of the company using ordinary, very common, most-likely-to-be-used-in-real-life hacker techniques. A data-driven defender cares about the current and most likely future successful local threats more than anything else.

After collecting and reviewing the data, it was great to give the CSO a ranked, prioritized, list of what we needed to fix first, based on current and future most likely attacks. He saw the value and required that all future unranked "fix it" lists be ranked with data before bringing them to him or his team for review.

Implementing a Thousand Security Controls

One customer wanted to implement every Microsoft security best practice configuration, which at the time numbered over 1,400 separate configuration controls. Most of them were defaults and highly likely to be already implemented. But a few hundred of them were likely to be "net new" in the environment, and it was expected that some far lower number of new controls, say less than two dozen, could be expected to cause some amount of operational interruption.

I was called in to assist with figuring out which controls were likely to cause the most problems, so we could troubleshoot them, try to minimize the pain, and get all the security controls implemented. My first question was "Which security controls will have the most value to the organization in minimizing the most current and future most likely successful threats?" Again, this organization already had a data-driven culture and could answer what the biggest threats were: Unpatched software and social engineering.

I performed an analysis of the 1,400 plus security controls and found only three that would have any bearing whatsoever on the top threats. I found that almost all the rest would provide nearly zero value for the organization in reducing current risk.

They either would be pushing out values that were already the confirmed defaults or would have zero impact to the organization's security risk against the real threats they faced. So, instead of helping to push 1,400 controls, I convinced them to push the three controls that would give them the most bang for their buck. And only pushing three controls resulted in less unplanned operational interruption.

Further, I helped them realize that overall, even these security configuration controls would have very little value for their organization if they did not first get their unpatched software and social engineering threats under control. What is the value of pushing out something that will cause operational interruption if its net result is not measurably lower risk? That is what a data-driven mindset thinks about all the time.

The overall idea is that unranked lists of tasks and items should offend you. Replace unranked lists of tasks and items with a list of prioritized ones that are selected using good data that accurately reflects the organization's worst current and future most likely threats. And there are some projects that should not be done in their current form because they don't really help significantly minimize risk, especially if the larger risks are not already mitigated. You must think with a data-driven mindset all the time. Otherwise, you are more than likely being inefficient with your time and resources and those of your organization. Don't volunteer to be part of the bad army that was described in Chapter 1.

Chapter 9 described many Data-Driven Computer Defense examples that highlight company- and individual-level responses and projects. Use them to help move your organization to a better Data-Driven Computer Defense plan.

Chapter 10 will help you sell your data-driven defense plan and mindset to the rest of the organization.

10 Selling DDD

Chapter 10 describes how to help spread the concept of a data-driven computer defense across your organization. It assumes that not everyone will immediately see the value of a DDD plan. Chapter 10 is a road map to selling DDD to disbelievers.

> *"It is not the critic who counts; not the man who points out how the strong man stumbles, or where the doer of deeds could have done them better. The credit belongs to the man who is actually in the arena, whose face is marred by dust and sweat and blood, who strives valiantly; who errs and comes short again and again; because there is not effort without error and shortcomings; but who does actually strive to do the deed; who knows the great enthusiasm, the great devotion, who spends himself in a worthy cause, who at the best knows in the end the triumph of high achievement and who at the worst, if he fails, at least he fails while daring greatly. So that his place shall never be with those cold and timid souls who know neither victory nor defeat."*——Theodore Roosevelt

Moving an organization from a traditional computer security defense to a data-driven one isn't always easy. Even if the concept is completely accepted from the very beginning by everyone, it requires new ways of thinking, possibly new people, and new or modified tools and processes. And that's if you already have the organization and senior management agreeing that it's a laudable goal.

I always posted the above Teddy Roosevelt quote on the wall behind my desk for all my employees to see when I was in IT senior management. I did it to encourage them when it seemed sometimes that we were fighting a tough battle to improve computer security. One of my favorite employees, who decades later is still a friend, snuck in and scribbled "The coward lives to tell how the hero died!" beneath my quote during a particularly stressful project. I laughed when I saw it because he was as right as Teddy Roosevelt was.

Expect Critics—Change Is Hard

After teaching the benefits of a data-driven defense plan for nearly a decade, I'm used to critics. Many people don't believe in the core ideas, even after I have shown them the data to support the new plan and introduced them to other leaders who were former critics who became fans after implementing it.

I had one senior computer security leader at a Fortune 50 company counter to me "So what if you tell me the number one thing that is most successfully attacking my company? How would that change anything that I do?" Needless to say, I was dumbfounded. To me that's like asking why a scientist needs data to prove an experiment or why an insurance company needs actuaries.

I get it. Changing paradigms is always a mental challenge, even when presented with absolute evidence over a very long time that what you are currently doing is not working (i.e. we live in an Assume Breach world). However, this also describes the behavior of so many previous "darling-of-the-stock market" companies that eventually get delisted and go belly up.

What worked before no longer works or never worked, but the new, better supported facts don't change the opinion of many of the longest-serving senior leaders who were previously celebrated as past heroes for following the old ideas. They cut their teeth and rose through the ranks by doing what was recognized as working even though it really didn't. It's hard to change, period, but even harder to change when your ego and career success were built on those old ideas.

It takes courage for an existing leader to be open to paradigm-shifting changes, even when shown good data to support the change. It's easier for someone with less exposure to the old way of something to readily make the shift. They don't have years and years of experience with the old system. They have less to question and fewer assumptions to throw away.

Every human being is potentially susceptible to resisting change, even those who think they are mentally prepared for change. This includes me. For example, if you would have come to me a few years ago and said you were going to spend hundreds of millions of dollars to make a service that would allow users to send a picture to other people that would only stay around for 15 seconds before it self-deleted, I would have called you a madman. That multi-billion-dollar service is called Instagram and is even more popular than Facebook with the younger crowd.

Similarly, I would have quickly rejected your idea to spend hundreds of millions of dollars to make a video service that capped videos at a maximum of six seconds. I would have replied that no one would watch those short videos, that nothing meaningful or exciting could be communicated in six seconds, and in any case, you can already post short videos, if you like, on YouTube. That was before I heard of Vine. In 2013 it was the number one downloaded app and had over 200 million users. The top Vine video creators made "stupid money" (i.e.

hundreds of thousands of dollars per year) for making "sick", six-second, looping videos. It was valued in the billions at its peak. It ultimately was bought by Twitter for $30 million (and later discontinued). Thirty million doesn't sound like much these days for a popular startup, but it's still bigger than any paycheck I've ever received.

I'm 52-years old. I can't understand the concept that not only are people being paid hundreds of thousands of dollars to play video games (i.e. e-sports), but that tens of millions of people will pay good money to watch them play. They have their own teams. Their own franchises. A younger relative of mine explained it to me this way: "We can't understand how you can watch slow baseball or football on TV. Our 'sport' is faster, more exciting, and more interactive than anything they could ever do. We feel the same excitement watching a good gamer play a game as you do watching your favorite sports star. Same feeling." I still don't get it.

And I don't get someone questioning the value of using better data to help better craft a more specific and efficient defense. How can someone argue against better data? When I'm flummoxed by data-driven defense critics, I try to remember this other quote perfect for the situation:

> "...*Propose to a man any principle, or an instrument, however admirable, and you will observe the whole effort is directed to find a difficultly, a defect, or an impossibility in it. If you speak to him of a machine for peeling a potato, he will pronounce it impossible: if you peel a potato with it before his eyes, he will declare it useless, because it will not slice a pineapple.*"—Charles Babbage, considered the father of modern computers

I understand that newness and change is hard. Paradigm shifting wouldn't be called "paradigm shifting" if it wasn't for a majority of the people not initially believing in something. If everyone immediately believed in something without asking for proof, it would be called "common sense", not a "paradigm shift". Paradigm shifts take years to take root, after which they come to be seen as common sense.

At least when I see the data that tells me I'm wrong, such as the growing market share of people simultaneously watching gamers while nearly every other traditional professional sport loses market share, I can change my thinking. Some people can't.

Human beings in general are resistant to change even when presented with good data. Today, there are security defenders who, when they hear that the old password policies that they've been following for decades are bad advice and are likely to be causing more hacking events, simply cannot believe it. They will have to be dragged kicking and screaming into making the necessary changes to their existing password policy.

My readers are the exception. I know that the very reason that you are reading this book is because you are open to new ideas and approaches. But that will not be true for everyone you encounter on your path to being a better data-driven defender.

The Benefits of a Data-Driven Computer Defense

This section is dedicated to describing the key benefits that can be expected with a Data-Driven Computer Defense plan. You can use these benefits in promoting Data-Driven Computer

Defense and justifying changing your company's existing defense paradigms.

The key benefit is more specificity and accuracy across all computer security realms, which produces a more efficient and productive defense. The following sections examine the key individual benefits of a data-driven computer defense approach.

More Intelligent Threat Intelligence

Improving threat intelligence focuses more on current, local threats followed by your most likely threats, which leads to a far better picture of your organization's real risk than what traditional threat intelligence provides. Improved threat intelligence results in better information that can be used to directly apply the right mitigations to the right problems. A data-driven defense saves time, money, resources, and many times the entire game.

Better Threat Detection

It's impossible to detect everything perfectly all at once, so you concentrate first on better understanding and then detecting the top threats. Fortunately, data-driven defenders tend to be better detectors for every threat overall because they understand root cause exploits and how important they are to the overall defense. Better detection of more root cause events helps to reduce risk of all events, top threats or not.

Coordinated Enterprise Security Strategy

Before a data-driven defense existed, no one could accurately state what the top most damaging threats were, supported by data. But a Data-Driven Computer Defense answers that question and then focuses the entire organization toward mitigating the top concerns. Previously, the organization might have been mistakenly using the disorganized army defense discussed in Chapter 1. Now it's a well-oiled machine with direction and purpose. It focuses on mitigating the top threats until they are no longer the top threats.

Improved Risk Assessment

There is a gulf of difference between the most critical potential threats and the most likely successful threats, and the difference matters more than everything else. There are tens of thousands of individual vulnerabilities and tens of millions of malware variants to worry about. But the ones you should react to the most and fastest are the ones that are currently damaging you the most and most likely to successfully damage you the most in the future. Everything else is a much lower risk equation.

Risk Assessment Is Risky

One caveat when trying to win the game of computer security defense is that it's important to note that risk assessment is always a risk in itself. Risk assessment tries to predict what threats an organization is most likely to be exposed to in the future. Any risk assessment assumes the risk that the predicted threats and risks might not align to the actual risks and threats that occur in the future. If earthquake preventers knew exactly where and when earthquakes would hit, we could just temporarily move the houses and buildings.

In fact, it's almost guaranteed that any risk assessment will not be 100% accurate. Threats and risks rise and fall over time. New threats arrive and older threats disappear. Even if you mitigate 100% of your predicted risks, an unexpected threat vector or determined adversary might penetrate your deployed defenses. Risk assessors understand their predictions might not always adequately protect their organization. But all other factors being equal, a risk-assessed defense that is based on real data should be more accurate than a computer defense plan that is based on "gut" feelings lacking collected data.

In the Florida Keys, where I live, we don't know when or where the next hurricane will hit, but we know how to build our houses so they have the best chance of withstanding a hurricane and which defenses are best for saving a house or a building. A hurricane might exploit some other weakness, but we look at the data and enforce the laws that make the most sense to save lives and prevent property damage. The same thing is true in computer security. You make your best guesses based upon previous history.

Better Computer Security Communication and Education

A data-driven computer defense plan puts the entire organization on the same page, focusing on the top threats, and accomplishes this by using better communications and education. A data-driven defense plan communicates to all stakeholders at their needed level of detail with more focus. Low-risk threats and random, unnecessary information are removed. What is left behind and driven home, again and again, is the organization's biggest threats. Everyone is on the same page.

More Efficient Defenses

When you understand the real, most damaging threats, you can begin to devise more efficient plans to stop them. When you're not sure what those threats are, maybe you mitigate the right things, and maybe you don't. When you have highly improved threat intelligence and threat detection, you can absolutely respond to the right threats with the right mitigations in the right amounts at the right time.

Quicker Response to Emerging Threats

The top threats change over time. The average company takes two to three years to appropriately respond to an emerging threat. A data-driven defense is built to look for increasing trends and to respond to them more quickly. Because data-driven defenders have real data tied to current, actual, successful exploits, they are able to respond to them more quickly than if they had no data at all.

Better Security Metrics

A data-driven defense plan uses better security metrics. Instead of using less useful metrics, like the total number of malware programs detected and removed, it measures the higher real risk, which is the mean-time-to-detect between when a malware program arrives and is detected and cleaned. A data-driven defender is forced to create or capture metrics that more accurately reflect the true risk in any environment. A data-driven defender is asking better questions to get better data and outcomes.

Accountable Defense Outcomes

A data-driven defense requires that all mitigations be measured and their success or failure at accomplishing what they were intended to mitigate be predicted and measured. If a particular mitigation fails to accomplish what it was proposed to do, the sponsor or vendor can be held accountable. Accountability also gives incentive for the sponsor to make sure the mitigation is well planned, correctly implemented, and operated optimally to prevent an inefficient outcome. A sponsor pushing less reliable mitigations will be discovered sooner and be given less trust over time.

Measurably Lower Risk

Lastly, and the whole reason we're doing this, is to show measurably lower risk. A data-driven defense measures the top current and most likely future SUCCESSFUL threats, and it does so by assigning metrics to them. By concentrating on the biggest threats that consume the largest amount of risk, a risk manager can clearly see the rise and fall in overall risk. Most defense plans can't show or measure risk at all. With a data-driven defense we are not only measuring, but measuring as accurately as is possible.

Happier Computer Security Employees

Inefficient computer security defense is exhausting and demoralizing. Nothing brings together an infighting community more surely than the focus on a common enemy. We would all be happier employees if we had clearer direction and communication toward the most worthy, common goals. Want to make your employees, co-workers, and bosses happier? Implement a Data-Driven Computer Defense.

Building Consensus

Moving to a data-driven defense usually requires consensus-building followed by the actual changes. With that expectation set, getting your organization from a traditional defense to a data-driven one usually involves two distinct phases: building consensus and operational transition.

I would love to believe that everyone, upon seeing the theory behind a Data-Driven Computer Defense, immediately sees the logic and readily adopts it. After all, who can argue with using better data to make more informed decisions?

Unfortunately, my nearly ten years of experience discussing and selling it shows me that it gets accepted like any other paradigm shift, meaning it has enthusiastic early adopters, followed by a growing number of further early adopters and then late adopters. Some implementers will have to be dragged kicking and screaming into a new paradigm, regardless of the data or successes. I don't take offense. It's a normal part of any innovation (https://en.wikipedia.org/wiki/Diffusion_of_innovations) and follows the technology adoption lifecycle (https://en.wikipedia.org/wiki/Technology_adoption_life_cycle).

I've even seen employees who either quit or essentially let themselves be let go because they refused to adopt the new paradigm reality. It's to be expected as a possible outcome. Change is hard.

The following sections explore what you can do to help build consensus and increase early adopters.

Education

Start by introducing all the relevant computer security defense planners to the concept of a data-driven defense. You can do this by passing around a copy of this book, downloading the free, earlier, originating whitepaper (https://gallery.technet.microsoft.com/Fixing-the-1-Problem-in-2e58ac4a), or presenting the related PowerPoint slides (https://www.linkedin.com/feed/update/urn:li:activity:63471799 71697475585).

There are also plenty of free Data-Driven Computer Defense–related articles from my 15+ years of writing for *InfoWorld* magazine and *CSO* (http://www.csoonline.com/author/Roger-A.-Grimes/). I sometimes post new content and related articles on my Twitter (@rogeragrimes) and LinkedIn (https://www.linkedin.com/in/roger-grimes-b87980111) accounts. I'll also gladly take questions at my personal email account (roger@bannerets.com).

I find that showing people the PowerPoint slides or the whitepaper followed by the book has the most immediate impact. As always, the best education is showing co-workers and employees your own demonstrated successes. It also can't hurt to share that many of the data-driven projects and outcomes will be of low or no additional cost. These projects often simply require a refocusing of existing resources.

Gain the Trust of Risk Managers

A Data-Driven Computer Defense is all about improving risk management. Ask existing risk managers how they currently determine cybersecurity risk assessments and likelihoods. Traditionally, they are calculating risk based upon criticality ratings given to them by IT security, which in most cases isn't adjusted for local threat experience.

Educate your risk managers first, asking if it would help them do their job better if they could more accurately and efficiently measure the top threats and the real risks they present. It's hard to find a risk manager who would not say "yes" in response. In my experience, risk managers get excited about the idea of using more relevant local data to drive more accurate risk assessments. I've had more than a few risk managers tell me they've long worried about the gap in accuracy of threat forecasts. In most cases, risk managers are early adopters of data-driven defense ideas, and they can significantly help you push its adoption to the rest of your organization.

However, pure risk managers aren't the experts in improving threat intelligence, improving threat detection, or selecting the right defensive mitigations. It's up to IT security personnel to work alongside the risk managers to get the entire data-driven defense lifecycle plan pushed out. Still, you'll usually find your risk managers to be among your biggest proponents if you introduce them to the concepts and talk about your plans.

Gradual Adoption

The person who coined the expression "You eat an elephant one bite at a time" was certainly someone with project management or leadership experience. It is difficult to go from zero implementation to full and complete adoption in a single step. Instead, plan for a gradual adoption process, starting with the "low hanging fruit", easy wins, and small proof-of-concept projects.

If you have data identifying what your most damaging current and future most likely threats are, you can more easily drive everything and establish early wins. When you have that, you can implement almost any other part of the data-driven defense lifecycle in ways that make the most sense for the organization. Even then, start with "baby steps", going for the easiest, most obvious wins. Nothing breeds broad cooperation like previous successes.

Personal Adoption

Assuming I have convinced you of the importance and necessity of a Data-Driven Computer Defense, you should start to live its credo in any way that you can. Chapter 9, "More

Implementation Examples", gives many examples that you can choose from in starting your own personal implementation.

I find a great starting point to be the example of using the current and most likely threats to drive criticality rankings of vulnerability scanning tools. This approach is one of the easiest to perform and the best examples for convincing others. When you see a big list of "high priority" items to fix, discuss what it would take to find out what the true top priorities are. Whenever given an unranked list of top priorities, push back a little to have it better prioritized by your organization's actual experiences.

> Note: Even if your current organization doesn't understand the importance of implementing a Data-Driven Computer Defense plan, your career can only benefit by adopting the key tenets. Thinking in a data-driven way will often make you the most sensible defender sitting at any discussion table. It will make you more valuable to any organization you work for.

Use small successful data-driven projects to drive broader consensus and support. With a few documented successes, you should have support from every level of the organization.

Operational Transition

Once you have broad consensus and senior leadership support, it's time to move to a Data-Driven Computer Defense plan and lifecycle. Follow the lifecycle steps enumerated in Chapter 8, "The Data-Driven Computer Defense Lifecycle".

Hold a Kick-Off Meeting

Now is the time to hold a kick-off meeting to get everyone on the same page. While bringing everyone up to nearly a common understanding is a key objective for the meeting, also listening to other participants and their data-driven suggestions is another. You want people walking out of the meeting feeling that they were clearly communicated with, they understand the forthcoming tasks and deliverables, and they can brainstorm and recommend suggestions. If you do it right, they will be energized or at least cautiously optimistic.

Hire More Data Analysts

In most cases, broader support and deploying a data-driven defense means hiring more data analysts or refocusing existing ones. Data is king and data analysts are royalty. Have the data analysts map out all the existing data, databases and their fields, links, relationships, input points, and outputs. You want your data analysts understanding all the existing data, where it is, and how they can access it.

Figure out the Right Questions

Ask each defense person or team to figure out what questions, if better answered, would help them to provide better defenses. For example, what is the mean-time-to-detect for malware? What are the top successful threats to line-of-business applications? How many databases are protected using encryption? How many laptops have encrypted drives? Is removable media encrypted? How can we detect pass-the-hash attacks? How far do computers "drift" away from their original configurations? What group policy settings give the most bang for your buck? What Internet browser is successfully compromised the most and why? What Internet browser app is involved in most successful compromises? Would smartcards or two-factor authentication significantly reduce attacks? Would application control whitelisting significantly reduce attacks? And so on. You want to figure out the best questions that, if answered, would lead to significantly reduced security risk. This is a time for brainstorming and analysis.

Improve Threat Intelligence

A data-driven defense starts with improved threat intelligence. Threat intelligence should be driven by local, successful (i.e. most damaging), current and future most likely threats.

Select Top Threats/Risks

Once the most damaging current and future likely threats are known, they should be prioritized and ranked. Do they share root exploit causes? How much of the overall organization's risk do they encompass? What critical assets can hackers ultimately access? All these factors must go into selecting the top threats.

Perform Gap Analysis

Where are the gaps, in threat intelligence, threat detection, risk ranking, metrics, communications, and data? One way to more easily see the gaps is to use a simple spreadsheet view with threats on one axis and the other components (e.g. threat intelligence, detection, etc.) on the other axis. Then rate coverage from 0 (completely missing) to 5 (adequately covered). You might even want to include a 6 (for overcovered).

Improve Threat Detection

Once you understand your right-aligned, risk-ranked top threats, now is the time to make sure they are adequately detected in your organization (according to the gap analysis). Add new detection methods where needed.

Improve Communications and Education Across the Enterprise

Communicate the top prioritized threats across the organization. Make sure that each piece of end-user education is first dedicated to mitigating the top issues. Each time that end-user education is used, make sure it focuses relentlessly on the number one threat until it is no longer the number one threat. And when it's time, repeat the process with the next new number one.

Select Metrics
Now that you know the top risk-ranked threats, select the metrics that will adequately measure their presence (or eradication) in your environment. If there isn't a good metric, brainstorm a way of creating one. If you can't measure it, you can't fix it. Define what success looks like, ahead of time.

Select and Implement Mitigations
Select and implement the mitigations needed to minimize or defeat the top risk-ranked threats. Mitigations should give you the biggest bang for your buck across the organization and should focus on the top threats.

Require More Accountability
Require accountability for the sponsor and vendors of the applied mitigations. Did each mitigation help with its threat metric? If not, why?

Start the Data-Driven Computer Defense Lifecycle
A Data-Driven Computer Defense is a constant lifecycle that uses improved threat intelligence to more accurately measure the top most damaging current and most likely future threats. It sees emerging trends earlier, responds more quickly, and demands accountability for mitigations against the right threats.

Overall Objectives
In a nutshell, a Data-Driven Computer Defense can be boiled down to a handful of basic memes, which I have intentionally repeated over and over in this book. You may be tired of

reading them, but there is an important reason for this repetition. Make sure these concepts are reflected in your plan. Let's revisit them again.

Overall Goal

Your aim is to more efficiently align mitigations against the organization's most damaging current and future most likely threats. You want to apply the right mitigations in the right places in the right amounts against the right things.

Key Objectives

A Data-Driven Computer Defense is a methodology and framework that helps to allocate security resources more efficiently and to effectively mitigate the top root causes of IT security threats. If applied correctly, it more efficiently minimizes initial breaches and resultant hacker activities. It does this by focusing on objectives that:

- Improve data collection and analysis
- Collect better threat intelligence
- Improve threat detection
- Focus on root causes
- Improve enterprise communication and coordination
- Better align mitigations to the most critical threats
- Increase accountability

Other Key Points

Here are other central key points to keep in mind when implementing a Data-Driven Computer Defense:

- There is a world-sized gap between the most critical threats you POTENTIALLY face and the biggest successful threats you ACTUALLY currently have and will most likely need to deal with in the near future.

- Local current exploit experience is the most relevant experience to your risk calculation, followed by mostly likely future threats. Everything else is a distant third.
- A few top threats/risks are likely to be the vast majority of your risk, and the rest of everything, all summed up together, usually doesn't amount to nearly as much.
- Focus more on root causes. An adware program takes just as much effort to exploit a computer as the most complex, backdoor, data-stealing, polymorphic Trojan horse program.
- Data is the conduit of success.
- Learn to ask the right questions.
- If you can't measure it, you can't rank or manage it.
- Work to create 10 to 20 "perfectly" accurate threat detection scenarios as a way to generate better threat detection.
- Gut feelings should be backed up by data. Data is king!
- There should be no more unranked lists.
- Communicate about the top threat until it is no longer the top threat.
- There is no right or wrong way to implement a Data-Driven Computer Defense in practice. Use what works in your environment and ignore whatever doesn't.
- A Data-Driven Computer Defense is best thought of as an attitude or culture, where good data is used to drive computer security decisions. Use it as a guiding principle.

Continue to Practice Defense in Depth

As discussed in Chapter 8, "The Data-Driven Computer Defense Lifecycle", just because most of your efforts should be focused on the top threats, that doesn't mean that you shouldn't be doing the other necessary "defense-in-depth" items that normal IT departments already do. A data-driven defense is about changing focus and priorities, not getting rid of the rest.

The best way to help move your organization to a better Data-Driven Computer Defense is by pursuing more easily achievable demonstration projects and showing success. Success breeds success. Start by asking the right questions and collecting the right data. Use that information to improve your organization's threat intelligence, threat detection, and recommended remediations. All of this should help you more efficiently align the right mitigations in the right places in the right amounts against the right threats.

Chapter 10 has explored how to sell and operationalize a data-driven defense in your organization.

Closing

In closing, I want to thank you for dedicating the time to read this book and giving a Data-Driven Computer Defense its long overdue consideration. I am convinced that every organization, person, and defense can benefit from adopting a more focused, data-driven mindset. Keep up the good fight and be a super-soldier in a better army!

Feel free to send questions and comments to me at roger@banneretcs.com.

Recommended Related Reading

Schneier, Bruce. *Beyond Fear: Thinking Sensibly About Security in an Uncertain World*, Copernicus Books, 2003

Boose, Shelly. "Key Metrics for Risk-Based Security Management" (http://www.tripwire.com/state-of-security/risk-based-security-for-executives/risk-management/key-metrics-for-risk-based-security-management/), *The State of Security*, July 2013

Jacobs, Jay and Rudis, Bob, *Data-Driven Security: Analysis, Visualization and Dashboards* (http://www.wiley.com/WileyCDA/WileyTitle/productCd-1118793722.html), Wiley, 2014

Microsoft Security Intelligence Reports (https://www.microsoft.com/sir)

Pereira, Marcelo. "Human and tech flaws caused data hemorrhage from Dept of Energy. Let's learn from their mistakes in 2014" (http://secunia.com/blog/human-and-tech-flaws-caused-data-hemorrhage-from-dept-of-energy-lets-learn-from-their-mistakes-in-2014-388), January 2014

Platt, Mosi K. "Making Your Security Metrics Work for You" (http://www.pivotpointsecurity.com/techno/security-metrics), Pivot Point Security, August 2012.

Symantec. "Why Take a Metrics and Data-Driven Approach to Security?", *Confident Insights Newsletter*, December 2012.

Young, Lisa. "Tips for Using Metrics to Build a Business-driven Threat Intelligence Capability" (http://www.isaca.org/About-ISACA/-ISACA-Newsletter/Pages/at-ISACA-Volume-18-27-August-2014.aspx), ISACA, August 2014.

Doerr, John. *Measure What Matters*, Penguin Random House, 2018.

Index